CH
ISLANDS
in your pocket

Travel Publications

Main Contributor: Christopher Catling

Photograph Credits
All photos supplied by The Travel Library:
7, 111; Stuart Abraham back cover, 26, 30, 33, 34, 35, 36,
42, 43, 45, 48, 49, 52, 54, 55, 76, 83, 95, 103, 109, 110,
119; Peter Balshaw 16; Stuart Black front cover, title
page, 10, 12, 21, 24, 25, 27, 29, 31, 32, 38, 40, 44, 46, 47,
51, 53, 57, 58, 60, 96, 105, 114; Philip Enticknap 4, 23,
63, 65, 67, 69, 70, 71, 74, 75, 87, 88, 90, 91(t,b), 125;
R Richardson 61; Peter Rouillard 15, 66, 72, 73, 77, 79,
81, 84, 86, 89, 94, 107, 116.

*Front cover: Mont Orgueil, Jersey; back cover: typical green
lane, Jersey; title page: costumed girl at the Battle of Flowers,
Jersey.*

MANUFACTURE FRANÇAISE DES PNEUMATIQUES MICHELIN
Place des Carmes-Déchaux – 63000 Clermont-Ferrand (France)
© Michelin et Cie. Propriétaires-Éditeurs 1999
Dépôt légal Mars 99 – ISBN 2-06-652701-7 – ISSN 1272-1689
No part of this publication may be reproduced in any form
without the prior permission of the publisher.
Printed in Spain 1-00/2

MICHELIN TYRE PLC
Travel Publications
The Edward Hyde Building
38 Clarendon Road
WATFORD Herts WD1 1SX - UK
☎ (01923) 415000

MICHELIN TRAVEL PUBLICATIONS
Editorial Department
One Parkway South
GREENVILLE, SC 29615
☎ 1-800 423-0485

CONTENTS

Introduction *4*

BACKGROUND
Geography *6*
History *9*
People and Culture *17*

**EXPLORING THE
CHANNEL ISLANDS**
Must See *20*
Jersey *24*
St Helier *24*
Eastern Jersey *38*
Lillie Langtry *42*
Central Jersey *44*
Western Jersey *49*
The North Coast *55*
*Jersey Zoo and
Gerald Durell* *60*
Guernsey *62*
St Peter Port *62*
Victor Hugo *68*
Southern Guernsey *70*
Northern Guernsey *78*
Herm *82*
Sark *85*
Alderney *91*

**ENJOYING YOUR
VISIT**
Weather *96*
Calendar of Events *97*
Accommodation *98*
Food and Drink *103*
Shopping *106*
Entertainment and
    Nightlife *108*
Sports *108*

A-Z FACTFINDER
The Basics *110*
A-Z Information *112*

Index *127*

INTRODUCTION

The Channel Islands are full of delightful anomalies. Though part of the British Isles, they lie just off the coast of France and enjoy warm and sunny weather for much of the year – quite unlike mainland Britain. The islands have their own laws, governments and ancient feudal practices. They pay no allegiance to Brussels or Westminster, being part neither of the European Union nor of the United Kingdom. Income tax is low and the islands act as a magnet to the wealthy. Goods are not subject to VAT and duty-free

shopping is all part of the fun of a Channel Islands holiday.

Petrol and car hire prices are among the lowest in Europe, so exploring the islands is cheap and easy. You can also escape the car entirely: the big islands have excellent bus services, while the lesser islands – tiny Sark and even more minuscule Herm – are completely traffic-free. Transport here, if you need it, is provided by bicycle or horse-drawn carriage. Even Jersey, Guernsey and Alderney are best explored by bicycle or on foot: some of the best beaches are accessible only by following the high-banked 'Green Lanes' that criss-cross the islands, or by descending down steep cliff paths where wild flowers bloom in profusion and seabirds nest relatively undisturbed.

The drive across the narrow isthmus of La Coupée, on Sark, is exhilarating and the highlight of a visit to the island.

The wonderful beaches, with their crab-filled rock-pools, clean sands and exotic shells, make the Channel Islands a perfect destination for families. Equally appealing are the profusion of medieval castles and Second World War fortifications (some built deep underground), as well as such attractions as Gerald Durrell's world-renowned Jersey Zoo.

This is also a destination for food lovers, with lavish displays of fresh fruit and seafood for sale in the covered markets, and shops in St Helier and St Peter Port selling baguettes and fresh farmhouse cheeses, along with real Normandy cider and inexpensive French wines. The streets are lined with pavement cafés, and every village has a pub serving mouth-watering food, from simple fresh crab to plates heaped high with seafood – all part of the French-influenced lifestyle that adds to the rich and varied Channel Islands mix.

GEOGRAPHY

The Channel Islands lie to the north of the Gulf of St Malo, and to the west of the Cherbourg peninsula. Alderney is the northernmost, located some 128km (80 miles) south of Weymouth, on the south coast of England, and 14.5km (9 miles) from the Breton coast. Sail south for 36km (21 miles) and you would reach Guernsey, Herm and Sark. From here it is another 36km (21 miles) to Jersey. Continue south again and, after 70km (44 miles), you would reach land near the Breton port of St Malo.

The seas surrounding the islands are subject to some of the biggest tidal movements in the world – during the spring tides, the water can rise at a rate of 5cm (2in) per minute, varying by as much as 12m (40ft) between low and high tide. This effect is visible in the vast swathes of golden sand that are exposed at low tide and in the acres of weed-covered rock that appear on all sides. These rocks are a great hazard to shipping, and beachcombers need to be constantly aware of the tides as they explore the crab-filled rock-pools of the foreshore. Check low water times and venture out only in the two hours before and after.

The Bailiwick of Jersey

The Channel Islands are divided into two groups, called Bailiwicks, for administrative purposes, and they have a combined population of around 140 000 – the same number of inhabitants as the Isle of Wight, but with just half the land area – 194km² (75sq miles) in total.

The Bailiwick of Jersey consists of Jersey itself, and the rocky islets of Ecréhous and

The headland of Belle Hougue, Jersey, provides dramatic coastal walks, but do not attempt the descent to the prehistoric cave without a guide.

the Minquiers Reef (also known as The Minkies). Measuring 14.5km (9 miles) east to west and 8km (5 miles) north to south, Jersey is the biggest of the islands (population 80 000) and the most southerly (lying 100 miles south of mainland Britain). Much of the island is composed of pink and grey granite, which provides the island with an excellent and durable building material. The granite weathers to form a free-draining soil whose fertility has been enhanced over many centuries by the lavish use of *vraic* (seaweed) as a fertiliser, a practice that continues to this day.

From the dramatic cliffs at the northern edge of the island to the golden beaches of

the south, Jersey tilts towards the southerly sun like a giant solar panel. Farmers have long taken advantage of this sun-trap effect to produce early-season crops of the famous Jersey Royal potatoes. Jersey cows have also been selectively bred since the 1830s for their rich milk, used to produce ice-cream, butter and other dairy products.

Although half of the island's land is farmed, agriculture now employs only around 2 000 people (2.5% of the population) compared with the 6 000 who work in the finance industry. Since the 1960s, Jersey and Guernsey's low tax regime, political stability and ease of access have made the islands attractive to many international banks as an offshore base for trading on world markets.

No longer Normandy, not yet England, with a touch of Brittany: a garden surrounded by the sea.

The Bailiwick of Guernsey

The Bailiwick of Guernsey consists of the islands of Guernsey, Alderney, Sark, Herm and Jethou, along with the lighthouse rocks of the Casquets, and the uninhabited islets of Burhou and Ortac. **Guernsey** (population 60 000) is the second-largest of the Channel Islands, roughly triangular in shape and measuring around 11km (7 miles) wide and 14.5km (9 miles) deep. The island has its own famous breed of cattle – larger than Jersey's, with the same limpid doe-like eyes, but sandy coloured rather than black. Until recently, the island was famous for its 'Guernsey toms' – deliciously sweet early-season tomatoes. These are still grown in the island's many greenhouses (along with courgettes, calabrese, capsicums and cut flowers), but their place has been taken on many supermarket shelves by cheaper Dutch and Canary Island produce.

Like Jersey, the boom in offshore financial services and the low tax regime means that many islanders enjoy a wealthy lifestyle, with open-market houses routinely selling for £1million and the island's marinas full of expensive yachts. With the highest rate of car ownership per capita in the world, Guernsey nevertheless remains surprisingly rural, with pretty green lanes leading down to wooded valleys and sheltered coves.

Tourism is a major source of revenue for all the islands, but especially so for the three lesser islands. Charming **Sark** (5km/3 miles wide by 1.6km/1 mile long) has a population of 600, greatly swelled by summer visitors arriving on day trips from Guernsey, 14.5km (9 miles) to the west. **Herm** (2.5km/1.5 miles by 1km/0.75 miles, population 103), is even closer to Guernsey: thousands of holidaymakers every year make the short 20-minute journey from St Peter Port to the island's tiny harbour. **Alderney** (population 2 000) is the third largest of the islands (5.6km/3.5 miles long by 1.6km/ 1 mile wide) and the most northerly; most of its summer visitors come over from France, since the island lies a mere 14.5km (9 miles) from the Cotentin peninsula.

HISTORY

Prehistory

The remains of some of Europe's earliest people have been found at the internationally important site of La Cotte de St Brelade, on Jersey's south-west coast. The finds, now displayed in the Jersey Museum, date from a quarter of a million years ago, when Jersey was still attached to the mainland of Europe. They show that Jersey's earliest inhabitants lived in caves and had an ingenious method of survival: they herded mammoth and woolly rhino together and deliberately drove them to their death over the cliffs, eating the flesh and using the skins to clothe themselves.

Some 10 000 years ago, at the end of the last Ice Age, the melting ice sheet caused sea levels to rise, cutting the Channel Islands off from the continent of Europe. Jersey and Alderney remained attached to the continent for 2 000 years longer than the other islands, which is why they have animals and reptiles, such as moles and toads, that are not found on Guernsey, Herm and Sark.

By this time, our prehistoric ancestors had developed into sophisticated farmers with a highly complex social organisation. Whoever controlled the islands – whether a priestly caste or warrior overlords – was certainly able to command vast resources and manpower, as the islands' many passage

Stone vases, pendants and axes have been excavated from the Faldouet Dolmen, Jersey, which dates from 2500 BC.

graves demonstrate. From the oldest (at Les Fouillages, on Guernsey's L'Ancresse Common Golf Course), built around 4500 BC, to the best-preserved (La Hougue Bie, on Jersey, with its intact earth mound), a huge amount of human effort was deployed in creating these communal graves, using massive granite boulders. Further evidence of the islands' wealth can be seen in the beautiful Bronze Age (2250-70 BC) gold torque and socketed axes in the Jersey Museum.

Traders and Saints

As the peoples of Europe became more mobile, travelling far and wide by ship to trade their goods, the Channel Islands became a frequent port of call, and one of the most exciting archaeological finds of recent years is the Gallo-Roman boat discovered in St Peter Port. A reconstruction of the boat can now be seen in Guernsey's Castle Cornet Maritime Museum, along with samples from its cargo of pitch, pottery, bronze, glass vessels and quern stones.

Close links with the Gauls of northern France continued into the early Christian era. St Marculf came over from Brittany and converted the islands to Christianity in AD 538. From then on, the islands looked to Brittany for their religious leadership, and many parishes (such as St Helier and St Brelade) are named after the Celtic saints and hermits who founded small monastic cells on the remote islands.

Normans and Tudors

In 933 William Longsword, the second Duke of Normandy, annexed the Channel Islands. It was at this stage that the island's parishes

The Annunciation Scene – one of the delicate medieval frescoes in the Fishermen's Chapel, St Brelade, Jersey.

and churches began to take shape, as well as the manorial system and landholding patterns. In 1066 William the Conqueror overcame England and forged the first constitutional links with the British mainland.

All was well until 1204, when King Philippe II of France conquered Normandy. The Channel Islands remained free but faced the most decisive moment in their history – whether to stay part of Normandy, or whether to remain loyal to their 'Duke', the English King John. The people of the Channel Islands decided to stick with King John. In doing so, they gained valuable privileges, including the right of independent government. To this day, the islands remain subject only to the reigning monarch, and not to the British Parliament.

As well as privileges, the Channel Islands also paid a price: France was now the enemy and, for the first time in centuries, the islands faced a hostile coast. Castles and coastal defences were erected and the islands were besieged again and again, in the constant wars between England and France, until, in 1484, the Pope declared the Channel Islands neutral, enabling the islands to trade freely, even in times of war.

Despite this, the English Crown continued to defend the islands, using their most talented military engineer, Paul Ivy, author of *The Practice of Fortification* (1589) to apply Italian ideas to the construction of Castle Cornet, on Guernsey, and Elizabeth Castle, on Jersey. Ironically, these castles were so well designed and built that several times in their history – especially during the Civil War, and again during the Second World War – the castles were used against those they were intended to protect.

During the Civil War, Guernsey and Jersey took opposite sides. Guernsey sided with the Parliamentarians, and their Royalist governor successfully survived a nine-year-long siege from his base in Castle Cornet. Royalist Jersey, by contrast, sided with the king and gave refuge to Prince Charles for nine months after the defeat of the Royalist cause. In 1649, immediately following the execution of Charles I, Jersey declared his son, Charles II, as monarch, the first place in the realm officially to do so, some 11 years before the Restoration. Charles II never forgot Jersey's loyalty, and he later rewarded the governor, Sir George de Carteret, with the grant of lands in the English colony of Virginia, which we now know as New Jersey.

Trade and Piracy
Links between the Channel Islands and the New World were to grow ever stronger during the 17C and 18C as the

Newfoundland trade was established. When the British wrested Canada from the French, entrepreneurs from the Channel Islands began travelling to Newfoundland to fish the rich cod banks, selling their catch to trading enterprises along the eastern coast of America as they travelled southwards, picking up cargoes of spice, timber and sugar in the Caribbean and crossing back to trade these in Spain and Portugal in return for wine and citrus fruits. This three-way trade funded many of the wealthy houses that were built on Guernsey and Jersey at this time.

Equally profitable was 'privatising', whereby civilian vessels were officially licensed to attack and seize enemy ships, sharing in the resultant spoils. This form of officially sanctioned piracy made many a fortune in the Channel Islands, and ironically led to the rise of smuggling in England, for even as the British government was taxing luxury goods in order to fund its wars with France, the spoils of those wars (brandy, tobacco, perfume and lace) were being shipped from the Channel Islands to be smuggled in, duty-free, through the coastal towns of southern England.

The Battle of Jersey

Understandably, the French tried to recapture the Channel Islands on many occasions. In Jersey, an invasion force, led by Baron de Rullecourt, landed in 1781 and took the Governor by surprise, persuading him that they headed a force several thousands strong. He surrendered the island, but Major Francis Peirson, at the head of the Jersey Militia, refused to accept defeat and attacked the French in Royal

Square. The Battle of Jersey lasted a mere ten minutes and ended in the defeat of the French – but also the death of the gallant Major Peirson. The Battle of Jersey – the last battle ever to be fought on British soil – is widely commemorated on Jersey as a symbol of the islanders' determination to retain their independence.

Even so, their way of life was soon to come under attack from a different quarter. From the beginning of the 19C, along with political émigrés from Republican France, there came a huge influx of British officers, retired on half pay after Napoleon's defeat at the Battle of Waterloo. Irish labourers also came to the islands to work on harbour development projects and these English-speaking migrants had a profound effect on the island's culture, triggering steady erosion in the use of the island's Norman-French dialect. As early as the 1870s, education was based on English patterns and language. In 1900 English became the language of the States, the island parliaments; English currency superseded French in 1923.

One of the 18C Martello Towers built to defend Guernsey's coastline (at L'Ancresse).

Occupation and Liberation

The most recent invaders to challenge the freedom of the Channel Islands were the Germans, who occupied the islands from 1940 to 1945. This dark period in the

islands' history is commemorated by scores
of museums across the islands and by the
huge number of German defensive works,
built in the expectation that the British
would at some stage attack the islands.
During this time, there were many acts of
bravery and heroism, and accusations of
collaboration, which have left unhealed
scars among those who lived through the
war.

Most have learned to forgive and forget,
however, and the Channel Islands now
attract many German, as well as French and
British visitors, who come specifically to visit
the islands' many war-time relics.

After the war, the potato industry
recovered quickly. The Jersey Royal Kidney
Fluke, developed more than 100 years ago
and unique to the island, is now worth £24

*German troops
march down
Guernsey High
Street, July 1940.*

millions a year in exports to the UK alone. In the 1940s and 1950s, unemployed French labourers were imported annually from Brittany to take part in the labour-intensive potato harvest, and, since the 1960s, their place has been taken by Portuguese workers from Madeira and the mainland. Today's large population of Portuguese mostly work in the hotel and catering industry, as agriculture has become increasingly mechanised, and tourism and financial services have taken over as the mainstays of the island economies.

PEOPLE AND CULTURE

The Channel Islands have a legacy of tradition arising from their Anglo-Norman history. They owe their ultimate loyalty to the Duke of Normandy, the title by which they know the reigning monarch of England. When Channel Islanders drink a loyal toast, they raise their glasses to 'The Queen, Our Duke'.

Internal affairs are managed by the two island parliaments, known as the States Assembly, though the islands delegate to the Home Office in London decisions relating to defence and international affairs. The Assemblies are made up of elected senators and deputies, and the islands take a certain pride in reaching consensus decisions, proudly boasting that they have no political parties, prime minister or cabinet.

Despite their similarities, there is a great deal of rivalry between Jersey and Guernsey. Guernsey markets itself as the 'friendly island', with the unspoken implication that people on Jersey are a bit hard-bitten and citified. Each of the Bailiwicks has its own currency and its own incompatible phone cards, not to mention its own postage stamps and different-coloured letter boxes and phone booths. Only half in jest will you occasionally hear Jerseymen referred to as *crapauds* (toads) – because the toad is found on Jersey but not on Guernsey; returning the compliment, Guernseymen, with their slower pace of life, are dismissed as *ânes* (donkeys) by their bigger island rivals.

The local dialect, Norman French, was used widely on all the islands until the 20C, and continues to be spoken by older residents. Even so, French survives in many areas of Channel Islands life – especially in legal and government affairs – and the island lifestyle has much in common with that on the continent. The names of long-established island families are French, and the street names are bilingual (often a street with a very prosaic English name will have a far more descriptive French alternative – Hill Street, for example, is La Rue des Trois Pigeons in French, referring to an inn of the same name that once stood there).

In architecture, there are strong similarities between the islands, with many fine granite farmhouses dating from the 17C and 18C. Datestones above the main doorways are sometimes deceptive: it was traditional for newlyweds to have their initials and the date carved on the lintel stone, but the house itself might well be much older. Manor houses, one to each of the island parishes, can be distinguished from other wealthy properties by the presence of a colombier, or dovecote, such as the one at Hamptonne Country Life Museum (*see* p.46). Only manorial seigneurs were allowed to keep pigeons – feeding freely on their tenants' crops!

Today, wealth and privilege are signalled by the ownership of luxury cars, of which there are many on the two larger islands, despite speed limits which mean that they will never be tested to their full potential. With income tax at only 20 per cent, and no capital taxes at all, the islands attract many wealthy residents, of whom TV traveller Alan Whicker, writer Jack Higgins (author of *The Eagle Has Landed* and 15 other best-sellers), and actor John Nettles, star of TV's *Bergerac* detective series, are among the better known.

Strict limits are set on the number of residency permits granted, however, and the islanders are very conscious of the need not to swamp the islands with houses, which would only destroy the features that make the Channel Islands so appealing. One of these is the intricate network of rural 'Green Lanes' that criss-cross both islands, providing an escape route for horse-riders, walkers and cyclists from the busier main roads. Also designed for escape – quite literally – are the ancient sanctuary paths (*perquage*) that run from the parish church to the sea: those who took sanctuary in the church were escorted down these paths to a waiting boat and were given help so long as they swore to leave the island for ever.

Exploring these lanes is a good way to discover the rich wildlife of the islands, where chemical-free farming has allowed wild flowers to flourish, along with many species of butterflies and birds. The islands combine northern European flora and fauna with such Mediterranean species as the green lizard, plus some creatures that are unique to the islands, such as the Jersey bank vole.

MUST SEE

Jersey★★

Jersey has enough attractions to keep you busy for a week and leave you feeling as if there is still much more to do. Of natural attractions, there are scores of **beaches** to choose from, depending on whether you want wild waves for surfing (try St Ouen's Bay), gentle warm seas for family bathing (St Brelade's Bay or the Royal Bay of Grouville), rock-pools and caves to explore (Plémont Bay) or a good choice of watersports (St Aubin's Bay). For **coastal scenery**, the cliff path from **Grosnez★** to Sorel is hard to beat for sheer variety, taking in caves and castles, museums (such as the North Coast Visitor Centre) and such dramatic sights as the **Devil's Hole★**.

There are enough **coastal defences**, Second World War bunkers and **prehistoric dolmens** to fill several books: if you want to sample the best, make sure you take in **Mont Orgueil Castle★** and **Elizabeth Castle**, the **German Underground Hospital★** and **La Hougue Bie★**. All but the Hospital are run by the Jersey Museums Service, and you can buy a passport saver ticket that will save you money on entry to six of their sites, which also

Popular with families, the Royal Bay of Grouville, Jersey, with Mont Orgueil Castle behind.

include the **Jersey Museum★**, the **Maritime Museum and Occupation Tapestry Gallery**, and the **Hamptonne Country Life Museum★**. Last but not least, do not forget to set aside at least half a day to visit Gerald Durrell's world-renowned **Jersey Zoo★★**.

Guernsey★

Most of Guernsey's main attractions lie in **St Peter Port★★**, which is itself a town of great architectural interest (the Guernsey Information Centre has walk leaflets and information on guided walks organised by local historical societies). **Castle Cornet★** and the **Guernsey Museum and Art Gallery** will both occupy a couple of hours and are excellent for children and adults. They are run by the Guernsey Museums Service, who offer a discounted three-in-one ticket, which also includes Fort Grey, home to the Shipwreck Museum. Victor Hugo's extraordinary house, **Hauteville House★**, is not to be missed, and there are charming shops to explore in nearby Trinity Square and Market Street.

Touring the island, you will find the south coast beautiful and unspoiled, with well-signposted cliff paths providing access to such sheltered bathing **beaches** as Fermain Bay and **Moulin Huet Bay**, while the **Guernsey Folk Museum★**, in **Saumarez Park★**, should not be missed for its informative displays on rural life a century ago.

Sark★★

This small but exquisite island is a delight to explore, for motor vehicles are prohibited and the charmingly old-fashioned and unhurried way of life persists here. Hire a bicycle or take a horse-drawn tour to appreciate the relaxed and gentle pace of this attractive island, though the drive across the narrow isthmus of **La Coupée★★★** is breathtakingly exhilarating rather than relaxed. The view of the **Port du Moulin★★** from the clifftops north of **La Seigneurie★**, home of Sark's ruler, is splendid and the narrow, flower-clad lanes offer a refreshing contrast to the dramatic coastline with its cliffs, coves and caves.

Petit Bot Bay is just one of the delightful sheltered coves which nestle along Guernsey's coastline.

JERSEY★★

St Helier

St Helier is the capital of Jersey, and home to more than half the island's population. From a small market town, St Helier evolved into the island's main harbour when Elizabeth Castle was built in 1600, superseding Mont Orgueil as the residence of the island's governor. St Helier was not the most perfect spot for a harbour: the huge tidal range that is a characteristic of the Channel Islands has always been a problem for merchant shipping. Much loading and unloading had to be carried out by carts driven out to the moored boats

St Helier's attractive harbour is peppered with boats of all shapes and sizes.

across the sands, and when Queen Victoria and Prince Albert visited in 1846, Albert wryly commented, 'You Jerseymen always build your harbours on dry land.'

By 1853 the problem had been partially remedied with the completion of the appropriately named **Albert Pier**. Since then the docks have been extended further out into the sea on several occasions, most recently to accommodate the increasingly large ferries that connect St Helier with England and France. After a period of neglect, a programme of redevelopment work is now under way that will restore the harbour to its central position as the focal point of the town.

The first fruits of the redevelopment are now visible in the form of **Liberation Square**, with its bronze statue of animated Channel Islanders waving the Union flag in celebration of their liberation from Nazi occupation in May 1945. The memorial was unveiled by Prince Charles in 1995, for the 50th anniversary of the Liberation, and stands in front of the town's former railway station, now converted to form the offices of the Jersey Tourism information centre.

To the left is the town's bus station and beyond, on the cliffs above, the stout granite walls of the 19C **Fort Regent**, now protecting a large leisure centre and sports complex. Further round, the tall chimney of the town's main power station is a prominent feature on the skyline. Dominated by these massive structures, St Helier is not a

Islanders celebrate their freedom – Philip Jackson's Liberation *sculpture, in Liberation Square, St Helier.*

picturesque town, but it is one full of
character and of historical interest.

The Maritime Museum and Jersey Occupation Tapestry Gallery

Exploring the town's history begins across
the Esplanade, on the North Quay, where a
group of mid-19C warehouses were
converted in 1997 to create the **Maritime
Museum** and **Jersey Occupation Tapestry
Gallery**, two museums in one that will
appeal to adults and children alike. In the
dimly-lit Occupation Tapestry Gallery, 12
embroidered panels ranged around the

A panel from the poignant Occupation Tapestry, depicting the story of the Nazi Occupation.

*An extraordinary
exhibition evoking
the darkest hours
of the island's
history.*

room glow with rich colour, illustrating
major events in the period between the Nazi
Occupation of the Channel Islands in 1940,
and Liberation in 1945. Completed in 1995,
for the 50th anniversary of the Liberation,
each of the richly detailed panels was
produced by one of Jersey's 12 parishes. On
the walls above the tapestry, black and white
pictures are projected of Jersey during the
war, and the fourth side of the gallery is
screened off to create a mini cinema
showing a video of the making of the tapestry.

By contrast with the sober and reflective
mood of the gallery, the next-door Maritime
Museum is filled with the excited sounds of
children learning about wind, waves and
tides, with the aid of numerous hands-on
experiments. Every aspect of the sea is
covered in this packed museum, from
shipwrecks to the tidal pull of the moon, and
from marine life to the many ways in which
humans pollute this precious resource.

*The landmark
Steam Clock
sculpture, St Helier,
was created in
1997 from the
former steamboat,
the Ariadne.*

It would be easy to spend another hour or so just in exploring St Helier's **port**, with the help of guides available from the museum bookshop – there are numerous plaques and sculptures commemorating key events in St Helier's history, as well as historic craft to look at, not to mention the busy life of the modern harbour, with its commercial vessels, yachts and high-speed car ferries. One unmissable sculpture stands between the museum and the bus station: the colourful **Steam Clock** is made from the boiler and paddles of a former steamboat called the *Ariadne*.

Jersey Museum★

Crossing over to the right of the bus station, you will find the fascinating **Jersey Museum★**, housed in an elegant former merchant's house and 18C warehouse in Ordnance Yard. Plan to spend at least two hours here discovering the many facets of Jersey's history, starting with the overview provided by the 12-minute audio-visual show, and moving on to the main galleries, which address such themes as the geology, prehistory, agriculture, trade and government of the island. Children will enjoy the grisly details of the treadmill, cat-o'-nine-tails and noose from the island's prison, and adults will enjoy the displays of 19C costumes and the portrait by Millais of Lillie Langtry (*see* p.42) in the art gallery on the top floor. In the adjacent Merchant's House, children can ride a rocking-horse and play Victorian games in the nursery of this restored period house. Unusually for a museum, this one also has a gourmet-standard restaurant, where you may want to linger over lunch, or afternoon tea.

Victorian Architecture and Fort Regent

From the museum, turn right and first right again into Mulcaster Street, where you will see two highly ornate pubs, typical of the eclectic style of St Helier's Victorian architecture. On the right is the Lamplighter, with Britannia seated in colourful glory on the roof pediment, and opposite is the plainer Corinthian.

Next comes St Helier's **Parish Church**, known simply as the Town Church. Built in the 11C, the original church of rough boulders and granite blocks was given some attractively traceried windows in the 15C. Alongside the pulpit is a simple memorial to Major Peirson, the hero of the Battle of Jersey (*see* p.14).

A typical 19C bedroom is shown in the merchant's house, Jersey Museum, St Helier.

Beyond the church, in Hill Street, you will find the main departure point for **Le Petit Train**, a road train that leaves every 20 minutes for the **Fort Regent** leisure and entertainment centre. Also accessible on foot, Fort Regent is the perfect place to take children on wet days: one admission fee admits you to all the facilities, which include a swimming pool, fitness centre, skate park, sauna and steam room, sports hall and indoor adventure playground. In addition, there is an aquarium displaying examples of local and tropical fish, a vivarium housing amphibians and reptiles, and an exhibition on the history of the fort, which was constructed in 1804-14 against a feared French invasion by Napoleon. The rampart walls provide good **views★** across the town and west to St Aubin's Bay.

Fun for all the family, whatever the weather, in Fort Regent, a large leisure centre and sports complex.

Relaxing in the shade of the chestnut trees, Royal Square, St Helier.

Royal Square

The eastern end of the churchyard of the Parish Church leads out into the tree-shaded **Royal Square**, one of the most attractive and historically important squares in the town. This was the market-place for medieval St Helier, the spot from which new laws and public pronouncements were made. As the plaque in the pavement in front of the gilded statue of George II records, this was also the site of the brief but decisive Battle of Jersey, in which the courageous Major Peirson defended the island against French invaders in 1781, losing his life in the process. Patches on the wall of the Peirson pub, on the north side of the square, mark the spots where musket balls struck.

The most important of the buildings here are the **Royal Court House** (built in 1866 but decorated with the arms of George II from an older building of 1760), and the adjacent **States Chambers** (1887), seat of Jersey's legislative assembly. Members of the

public can visit the Chamber (entrance in
Halkett Place) and watch the proceedings
from the public gallery on Tuesdays, when
the House is in session.

Shops, cafés and markets

If you walk past the Peirson pub, you will
enter traffic-free King Street, at the heart of
St Helier's main shopping area, where the
streets are lined with shops and department
stores selling jewellery, wines, clothing,
electronic goods and souvenirs. Turn right,
to the junction of Queen Street and King
Street, with the ornate Mappin & Webb
building on the corner, and then left into
Halkett Place, where you will find one of
several entrances to St Helier's ornate
Central Market. This is a fine example of a
Victorian cast-iron market hall with a wealth
of decorative detail, especially around the
central fountain, where visitors throw coins
for luck. Built in 1822, the market has stalls

*St Helier's indoor
Victorian market is
full of colourful and
tempting displays of
food and flowers.*

selling fresh fruit and vegetables, cheeses, delicious French-style gateaux, fresh bread and a colourful assortment of cut flowers.

Heading through the market to Beresford Street, you can cross over to find the narrow entrance to **Beresford Market**. Here (daily except Sundays and Thursday afternoons) you will find stalls piled high with all the fish that can be found in Channel Island waters – including live crabs and lobsters, conger eel, and an array of cooked shellfish. Cafés in the market also serve fish to a mixed clientele of hungry shoppers and businessmen from nearby offices.

Broad Street and the Parade

To complete this tour of St Helier, return to Royal Square and leave by the western side of the square, past the former police station, with its sundial on the wall, and the ornately decorated premises of international banks. You will enter Broad Street, with its obelisk

And to complete the meal, fresh fish from Beresford Market.

memorial to Peter le Sueur, five times
Constable (the equivalent of mayor) of St
Helier in 1811-53. The main post office on
the left sells special issues of Jersey postage
stamps, and to the right is one of St Helier's
most popular shops, the Marks & Spencer
department store. Broad Street leads to
Charing Cross, with its Croix de la Reine, a
granite cross made in 1977 to commemorate
the silver jubilee of Elizabeth II. Turn right
into York Street, passing the pastel-painted
and flag-bedecked **Salle paroissiale** (Town
Hall), built in 1870 in French style.

Broad Street widens out to form **The
Parade**, so-named because this was the spot
where the island's military garrison once
held its parades. A Cenotaph,
commemorating the island's war dead, and a
memorial to the French Resistance, in the
form of a Cross of Lorraine, are dwarfed by

*Busy shoppers in
St Helier.*

the huge bronze memorial to General Don (Jersey's Governor in 1806-14), surrounded by cannon.

Take the first left, Gloucester Street, to pass the former workhouse of 1765, rebuilt as Jersey's General Hospital in 1860, on the right. Further down on the left is the boarded-up façade of the town's Opera House (opened in 1900 and rebuilt after a fire in 1921); there is an ambitious plan to restore the theatre once funds have been raised.

Gloucester Street leads back to the Esplanade where the **Jardins de la Mer** were laid out in 1997, with fountains and a walkway that offers fine **views** over to **Elizabeth Castle** (dramatically spotlit at night). To reach the castle, either you can walk across the 1000m (3 280ft) causeway from this spot (the causeway is uncovered for two hours each side of low tide, and the walk takes about 25 minutes), or you can take the ferry from the nearby West Park slipway, driving across to the castle in an amphibious vehicle.

Elizabeth Castle stands on a rocky islet where St Helier, the hermit and Christian missionary who gave his name to the island's capital, first settled in the 6C. Helier was murdered by pirates in 555, and a monastery was established in his honour soon after. The rock was not fortified until Paul Ivy, Queen Elizabeth I's military engineer, realised that it was perfectly positioned to

Costumed guardian of Elizabeth Castle, St Helier.

defend St Helier's harbour. The castle he designed was completed in 1600, when Sir Walter Raleigh first took up residence as Jersey's governor. In 1646, Charles II (then Prince of Wales) took refuge in the same Governor's House, and returned there in 1649 to be proclaimed king (though no other part of the British Isles was ready then to accept him as such).

Parliamentarians bombarded the castle from the mainland and succeeded in blowing up the munitions store, in the crypt of the abbey church, in 1651. The island's most ancient church was thereby destroyed, and only a granite cross now stands on the site of the church, surrounded by handsome pink granite barrack buildings, dating from the 18C rebuilding of the castle. These buildings now house a café and several

When the tide turns, take the amphibious DUKW across to Elizabeth Castle.

exhibitions. One tells the story of the castle and uses contemporary furnishings to contrast the life of the ordinary soldier, living several to a room in cramped barracks, and that of the officers in their luxurious rooms. Another explains how ever more deadly and accurate artillery resulted in the need to constantly rebuild and rethink the defences at Elizabeth Castle, and a third looks at the history of the Jersey Militia.

The final element in the castle's history was its re-use by German troops during the Occupation, and there are several casemates to explore, with their guns still in place, as well as the fire tower at the summit of the Elizabethan castle, commanding panoramic **views★** over the bay.

The Occupation Museum

Returning to the Esplanade from Elizabeth Castle, turn right to go back to Liberation Square. As you head off down the Esplanade, you will pass **The Occupation Museum**, on the left, facing the mural of a passenger steam train painted on the side wall of the former railway station, now the tourist information centre.

The Occupation Museum, like several similar museums on the island, brings home the hardships and privations suffered by the people of Jersey through the Occupation years. As well as an excellent 45-minute video, in which people who lived through the war tell their stories, the displays include photographs, newspaper cuttings, letters and documents, and objects, such as German military equipment, and the food parcels that were sent to the Channel Islands, in the final bitter winter of the war.

Eastern Jersey

After St Helier, the town that every visitor to Jersey ought to see is **Gorey**, with its Regency harbour and the perfectly poised Mont Orgueil Castle rising from a granite knoll. To reach Gorey, you can either take the A4 coastal road east out of St Helier and follow it all the way , or take the A5 road and call in at **Samarès Manor** along the route. Samarès Manor provides the only opportunity you will get on Jersey to see inside a stately home. Remodelled in the 18C, there are Norman remains in the undercroft to suggest that the manor goes back to the original conquest of the Channel Islands by the Normans in the 10C. The walled herb garden is packed with fragrant medicinal and culinary plants, and other attractions include a children's farm, craft centre, and falconry display.

The elegant Samarès Manor, whose impressive gardens were extensively landscaped in 1924.

From Samarès, turn left and then right on the B48 road to return to the coast where, if the tide is out, you will enjoy the eerie sight of the mass of hidden rocks and reefs that surround the shores of **St Clement's Bay**. Looking like a cross between a lunar landscape and a miniature version of the Arizona desert, the weed-covered rocks stretch as far as the eye can see. Rounding the south-eastern tip of Jersey, you will notice a run of defensive towers as you drive up the coast past the sandy **Royal Bay of Grouville**. They are among those built between 1179 and 1835 to defend the coast from French attack.

None compares in magnificence, though, to splendid **Mont Orgueil Castle★**, dominating the view as you approach Gorey, and described by Sir Walter Raleigh as a 'stately fort of great capacity'. Raleigh was given instructions to demolish the castle in 1600, after the residence of the governors of Jersey was moved from here to Elizabeth Castle, in St Helier. He successfully pleaded for its retention, and the castle was used as a state prison until the 17C. Waxwork tableaux, recalling key moments in the castle's history, are mounted in the main rooms of the keep, and there are magnificent **views★★** from the ramparts.

Gorey village lies just inland, and if you follow the signs you will come to the **Jersey Pottery**, one of the island's most successful craft enterprises. Visitors come here to see the pottery being made and decorated, but word has also got about that the restaurant, serving fresh seafood and home-baked pâtisserie, is one of the island's best for lunch, so you will find plenty of islanders here as well as visitors.

Just north of Gorey, off the B30, signposts direct you to the **Faldouet Dolmen**, a very well-preserved passage grave of around 2500 BC, originally covered with an earthen mound (*see* p.10). To see what the dolmen would have looked like, take the B28 westwards to La Hougue Bie, passing on the left the pretty **Queen's Valley Reservoir**, built as recently as 1986 (a delightful walk goes all the way round the water's edge).

Mont Orgueil Castle looms over the charming port of Gorey.

La Hougue Bie★ is one of Europe's most imposing passage graves. It is also one of the best preserved – of the thousands of such graves that have survived, almost all lost their covering mounds when treasure hunters and antiquarians dug them up in the 18C and 19C. Here excavation was carried out according to modern scientific principles in 1924, and the mound survives to the impressive height of 40m (123ft), crowned by a medieval **chapel**. The fascinating site encompasses the **Museums of Geology and of Archaeology**, a reconstructed **Neolithic hut**, and a spacious German **communications bunker**, but it is the mound itself that most enthrals visitors, with its womb-like interior, constructed around 3500 BC from massive blocks of granite.

Perhaps seeking to neutralise the pagan force of the tomb, the Normans built a small chapel, dedicated to **Our Lady of the Dawn**, on top of the mound. This was extended in 1520 by the addition of the **Jerusalem Chapel**, with its ceiling paintings of praying angels. Long after the mound's true antiquity had been forgotten, local people claimed it to be the burial mound of a brave Norman knight, the Lord of Hambye. Having slain a dragon that had been terrorising the neighbourhood, he fell asleep, only to be murdered by his own squire. The squire returned to court, claimed to have killed the dragon himself, and stated that the Lady of Hambye should marry him to fulfil his master's dying wish. When the squire later confessed all in his sleep, he was put to death and the mound at La Hougue Bie was raised over the true knight's grave.

Lillie Langtry – the Jersey Lily

Lillie Langtry, the vivacious and beautiful daughter of the Dean of Jersey, was born in St Saviour's parish in 1853. Having visited London as an 18th birthday treat, she resolved to escape Jersey, agreeing to marry Edward Langtry, a man of considerable wealth – or so it seemed. His wealth turned out to be less than his extravagant lifestyle suggested, but he provided Lillie's passport to London society, where her radiant character and perfect complexion inspired the poets and painters of her day.

Her famous 1878 portrait by Sir Edward Millais is entitled *The Jersey Lily*, a pun on her name and a reference to the nerine flower that she holds in her hands. Sir Edward Poynter's more sensuous portrait, of Lillie in a low-cut

dress of gorgeous red and gold, perhaps captures better the coquettish nature that enabled her to embark on a three-year affair with the Prince of Wales. Invited to every party, Lillie became one of London's Professional Beauties, her picture appearing daily in newspapers and magazines, and her taste in clothes setting the style that other women followed.

Lillie's life changed dramatically when the Prince of Wales turned against her, following a misjudged prank (Lillie dropped an ice-cream down his back at a ball, which the Prince interpreted as contempt for his person). Lillie was suddenly shunned by society, debts were called in and she was bankrupted. Friends persuaded her to go on the stage, where she quickly rebuilt her wealth. Her career took her to the US, where the *New York Times* railed against her lack of propriety in 'going beyond the bounds of good taste in unnecessarily removing her clothes on stage'. Despite, or because of, this, she enjoyed an immensely successful career, even starring in a silent movie in 1913, before retiring

to a secluded life in Monte Carlo.

Subsequent commentators have hailed Lillie Langtry as a pioneer of the right of women to lead an independent and unshackled life. Another perspective is provided by Ira Goldsmith, her secretary and companion, who called Lillie the 'saddest woman I have ever known – loaded with jewels and famous, yet many a night I have known her cry herself to sleep'.

Above Lillie Langtry's tombstone, in St Saviour's churchyard.
Left A selection of Lillie's jewellery.

The pretty church of St Saviour's is Lillie Langtry's final resting place.

An intricate network of rural 'Green Lanes' criss-cross both Jersey and Guernsey.

Returning to St Helier along the B28 and A7, stop at **St Saviour's Church** to see the grave of Lillie Langtry, marked by a beautiful bust of pure white Carrara marble at the far western end of the churchyard. The church also has some fine 15C tracery, filled with colourful stained glass. Also on the A7 road into St Helier is the **Photographic Museum**, in the grounds of the Hotel de France, with changing displays of historic photographs and period equipment.

Central Jersey

To explore central Jersey, leave St Helier on the A8. After 2 miles or so, you will pass the **Sir Francis Cook Gallery** on the left, housed in a converted Methodist Chapel and schoolroom (note that it may be closed off-season). The gallery shows work by local and overseas artists, including paintings by Jersey-born Sir Francis Cook. The A8 stands

between two scenic valleys, threaded by Green Lanes, ideal for walking. The pretty Valleé des Vaux stands to the east, and the Grands Vaux Reservoir to the west. In the lanes to the north of the reservoir, the late Eric Young created his **Orchid Foundation★** housing one of Europe's finest collections of these exotic rainforest plants. The Foundation continues to breed new hybrids, many of them given Jersey place-names. Raised beds in the display house show off the gorgeous plants to their best advantage, providing plant lovers with a feast of different shapes, scents and colours.

A little further up the A8, on the left, signs point to the **Little Loft Gallery and Turnery**. Here, a fine old Jersey farmhouse has been

Exotic blooms at The Eric Young Orchid Foundation.

converted into an art gallery displaying work by local artists, and the beautiful turned wood bowls and jars of the owner, Mick Renouf. It is a short step from the gallery to the sights, sounds and smells of the **Pallot Heritage Steam Museum**, with its working railway, displays of traction engines and theatre organs (trains run on Thursdays).

The Steam Museum is located almost at the very heart of the island. The **Island Centre Stone**, marking the exact geographical spot, lies in the hamlet of Sion, just to the south-west, among a network of quiet high-banked lanes so typical of Jersey's interior. The law of *branchage* imposes a duty on Jersey landowners to keep these lanes clear, so that branches and vegetation do not impede the passage of vehicles. This and other aspects of rural life on the island, are explained at the excellent **Hamptonne Country Life Museum★**, set in the verdant Vallée de St Laurens (now known more prosaically, because of its numerous reservoirs, as Waterworks Valley).

Hamptonne is a beautiful old farm complex, surrounded by high, sheltering walls of pink granite. A date carved on the roadside arch says 1637, but this was the year in which Laurens Hamptonne le Vicomte acquired the farm – some of the mellow thatched buildings here date as far back as the mid-15C, if not earlier. If you are lucky, your visit will coincide with one of the days when the 'goodwyf' is busy working in the main farmhouse, a costumed guide who will explain the history of the house and the daily farming routine. There is also a video, in which local people talk about their work

The mechanically-minded will enjoy the fascinating collection on display at the Pallot Heritage Steam Museum.

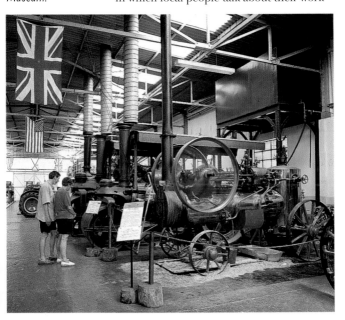

on the land, providing a nostalgic look back at the time, only a few decades ago, when Jersey had numerous small mixed farms, with a few cows and a few fields of potatoes, supplemented with tomato growing in summer and cider production in autumn. Nearly all have now given way to larger mechanised enterprises, specialising either in potatoes or in milk production.

Westwards into the next valley, the geology subtly changes from hard granite to softer compressed muds and clays. This shale landscape was exploited by the Nazis during the Occupation as the location for a massive complex of underground tunnels, dug by prisoners of war and equipped to provide a hospital for German casualties, in the event that the Channel Islands were ever attacked. The **German Underground Hospital★** is now one of Jersey's most compelling wartime attractions. Unfinished tunnels, left exactly as they were when they were discovered after

A tour of the German Underground Hospital can be an eerily realistic experience.

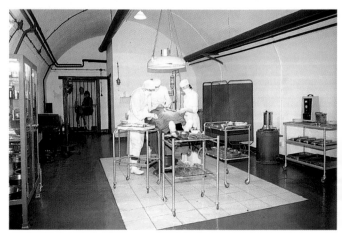

the war, bring home the sheer scale of the work involved in digging and equipping the tunnels, and the number of lives lost in the process. Three of the wards are now used to show videos, incorporating rare wartime footage (filmed at great risk to the local population, since camera ownership was punishable by death), telling the story of the Occupation. Other rooms, including the officers' mess, have been convincingly reconstructed according to their wartime appearance.

Returning to St Helier, look out at Millbrook for the whitewashed tower of **St Matthew's Church** (there is a large car park alongside). Known as the **Glass Church**, this light and airy church is full of moulded opaque **glasswork★** designed in the 1930s by the French artist, René Lalique, including a glass font, altar screen and windows. The magnificent work was commissioned by Lady Trent as a memorial to her husband, Lord Trent – perhaps better known as Jesse Boot, founder of the Boot's the Chemist store chain.

Detail from the art deco glasswork of René Lalique, at St Matthew's Church, also known as 'the Glass Church'.

Western Jersey

Western Jersey has some of the island's finest beaches, as well as a number of popular visitor attractions. One is the **Moulin de Quetivel**, a working water mill, reached by following the airport signs west out of St Helier, and taking the A12 north towards St Peter's. The mill is signposted off to the right and is hidden in the wooded **St Peter's Valley**. Six mills once lined the banks of the valley stream, but only Quetivel survives, first recorded in 1309 and restored to full working order by the Jersey National Trust.

Driving up St Peter's Valley along the A11 will bring you to a much more recent attraction, **The Living Legend★**. An all-too-short multi-media presentation tells the story of Jersey, mixing fact and legend into a thrilling half-hour entertainment, with volcanic eruptions, sea-storms and a noisy re-enactment of the Battle of Jersey to keep you on the edge of your seat (very young children may find the special effects too frightening). In addition, there are tableaux set around the deck of a cross-Channel steamer detailing various aspects of Jersey, from well-known residents to the singular laws of the island. Separate entry is charged for the Adventure Golf Course alongside, and there are various craft shops, cafés and playgrounds within the complex.

Jersey Motor Museum, further west in St Peter's village, is a place for nostalgic motor buffs, with its displays of lovingly maintained vintage cars. War memorabilia are displayed at the nearby **St Peter's Bunker Museum**, and both attractions stand close to **St Peter's Church**, whose French name, St Pierre dans le Désert, refers to the vast dune system that stretches all the way down the western coast of the island, providing space for several golf courses and a home for the island's colony of green lizards. Beyond the dunes lies **St Ouen's Bay** (pronounced 'Wons'), a 5km (3 mile) stretch of firm golden sand, perfect for sunbathing and popular with surfers, as well as joggers and sandcar-racers (races are normally held on Saturdays). Despite its

Shrimping by the Rocco Tower, St Ouen's Bay.

apparent calm, there are strong offshore currents, and swimmers should take heed of the lifeguards and warning signs.

The road south along the bay leads to **Corbière Point**, a wonderful and dramatic spot for walking, especially at sunset. A concrete causeway provides access, at low tide, to the **lighthouse**, and cliff paths invite walkers to explore the rocky coastline, with its German fortifications. By contrast with this wild spot, **St Brelade's Bay** is almost Mediterranean in ambience. The whole sweep of the seaside resort of St Brelade and the sheltered cove is visible from the rocky

Corbière lighthouse, built in 1874 to warn ships of this perilous stretch of water.

shelf to the west, where the medieval **Fishermen's Chapel** is located, alongside **St Brelade's Church**.

Archaeologists believe that St Brelade refers to St Branwalader, who established the first simple chapel here as a missionary from Brittany. Later on, the bigger parish church grew up alongside, and the atmospheric **Fishermen's Chapel** became a chantry chapel, where prayers were said regularly for the souls of the donors who paid for the delightful 15C **frescoes★** that decorate the whitewashed walls and pointed vaults. Pride of place is given to an *Annunciation* scene,

Areas of unspoilt heathland surround Portelet Bay.

where the donors are all depicted kneeling on either side of the Virgin and the Angel Gabriel (*see* p.12).

From St Brelade's, those interested in Second World War history should visit **Portelet Bay** and **Noirmont Point★**, for its German fortifications. Gentler and more fragrant sites await at the Jersey **Lavender Farm**, on the B25 east of St Brelade, especially when the flower harvest is in full swing in June and visitors can watch lavender oil being extracted for use in toiletries and perfumes (at other times of the year, a video explains the process). Call in at the **Shell Garden** if you want to give your children a treat, or go for a stroll along the firm sands of St Aubin's Bay to **St Aubin's Fort**, possibly medieval but now enwrapped by German fortifications. You may see people surfing, water-skiing or paragliding along the bay: if you want to join them, there is a watersports centre at La Haule, along the bay's western rim.

Fragrant work at the Lavender Farm.

Seeking inspiration for beach-combing expeditions in Shell Garden, decorated by its owners with imaginative shell designs.

The North Coast

Jersey's northern coast, with its steep cliffs punctuated by tiny coves, is entirely different in character from the southern and western coasts, with their broad sandy bays. You will see little of the north coast from the car, however. The roads stay inland and you must get out of your car and walk if you want to enjoy the coastal scenery – there are many clifftop paths to explore, overlooking rocky headlands where seabirds nest and waves dash against the rocky shores.

A tiny port, of doll's house proportion, where geese bask in the morning sun.

To explore the north coast, head out of St Helier on the A6 road, signposted to St Martin. Tiny **Rozel** is the first destination; named from *roseau*, meaning reed, the lush and sheltered bay has some notable gardens in the wooded valley behind (open occasionally for charity) and some of the island's best fish restaurants grouped

around the tiny shingle beach. **Bouley Bay** is the next cove, famed for its diving and fishing and backed by National Trust-owned woodland. Normally peaceful, hill-climb events staged on the steep road west of the bay can attract large crowds, as can **Jersey Zoo★★** (*see* p.60), just to the south.

Belle Hougue headland, to the west, is the site of Jersey's highest point (133m/435ft above sea level), unmissable for its forest of radio and telecommunications masts. More attractive is **Bonne Nuit Bay**; local legend has it that the name was bestowed by Charles II, as he escaped to France whispering 'Bonne nuit belle Jersey,' though in fact the name is recorded as early as 1160. The intriguingly named **Wolf's Caves** are reached by a steep cliff path to the west of the headland; 118m (350ft) deep and 18m (60ft) high, the cave is probably named after the *loup de mer* (sea wolves, or sea perch), caught by local fishermen.

Quarrying has eaten away at Ronez Point so that its neighbour, **Sorel**, is now claimed as Jersey's most northerly point. **Devil's Hole★**, further west, is a blow-hole surrounded by cliffs, created when a cave roof collapsed in ancient times. The modern bronze figure of the devil at the start of the path has replaced an older wooden one carved in the mid-19C from the figurehead of a ship wrecked here in 1851.

The road turns inland here and passes **La Mare Vineyards**, set in the grounds of a fine 18C house, where a video provides an introduction to the history of the estate and the wine-production cycle. Afterwards, visitors follow a trail around the farm before visiting the Vintry, where the wines are made, for a tasting. Try Clos de la Mare, Clos

Pretty as a postcard, Rozel Harbour is still a working fishing harbour.

de Seyval or Blayney Special Reserve, and you won't be disappointed. To the south, the **Jersey Butterfly Centre** has many exotic butterflies flying freely under glass, and a third local enterprise, the **Jersey Flower Centre**, provides a comprehensive account of the island's horticultural industry.

Best of all is the **North Coast Visitor Centre**, run by the Jersey National Trust, and housed in the 19C barracks, built above the sandy beach at **Grève de Lecq** to guard the coast from attack by Napoleon's troops. Fully restored, the barracks house several

horse-drawn vehicles and displays on the history and wildlife of the north coast.

Grosnez Castle, an older fortification, stands in ruins on the desolate **Groznez Point★**. Only a few walls now remain of the 14C castle, but there are superb northerly **views** to Guernsey, Sark and Herm. Nearby, at the western end of **Plémont Bay**, is the archaeologically important **La Cotte Cave**,

Wide, sandy Plémont Bay is backed by steep cliffs dotted with caves to explore.

one of several caves worth exploring here if tides allow.

Heading southwards and inland, back towards St Helier, you can take your pick of a number of attractions clustered around the northern end of St Ouen's Bay. The **Battle of the Flowers Museum** is an idiosyncratic but child-friendly display of prize-winning floats made for Jersey's annual carnival (*see* p.97). Most depict animals and birds and were created from grasses grown, picked, dyed and painstakingly mounted onto wire and wood frames by Florence Bechelet in the 1960s and 1970s. **Treasures of the Earth** takes visitors on a geological tour through mocked-up caves glistening with jewel-like minerals and gem stones, and includes a display of fossils.

The **Channel Islands Military Museum** shares a site with Jersey Woollen Mills (*see* p.108); the restored German bunker displays uniforms, motor cycles, military equipment and documentation from the Occupation era. **Kempt Tower**, set among the dunes of St Ouen's Bay, is a Napoleonic-era Martello tower now converted to an Interpretation Centre with a video theatre where you can learn about the coastal wildlife, while the nearby **Frances Le Sueur Centre** provides information on the rare plants, birds and reptiles of the adjacent **Les Mielles** nature reserve.

As you return to St Helier along the A12 you may catch a glimpse of historic St Ouen's Manor (not open to the public), home of the de Carteret family, whose members have played a key role in the island's history for more than 1 000 years. Just occasionally, the delightful manor gardens are open to the public for charity.

Jersey Zoo** and Gerald Durrell

The late Gerald Durrell (1925-95) established the Jersey Wildlife Preservation Trust in 1963 at a time when zoos were primarily designed for entertainment. The public wanted to be amused by the antics of the animals, and their welfare was a secondary consideration. Durrell turned this approach on its head, and his revolutionary methods have now become the standard by which all zoos are judged.

Durrell set out to create a refuge for animals that were facing extinction in their native habitat. Rescuing them from oblivion could never be a simple matter of breeding up the numbers in a zoo and then returning them to the wild. The zoo is merely one facet of a complex and costly programme of research designed to find out why the animals are facing extinction, and what aspects of their habitat, or of the animal's own behaviour, or of man's inter-relationship with the animals, need to be changed in order to give them a better chance of survival. Some of the creatures in Jersey Zoo – especially the shyer nocturnal animals – are so little understood that it takes years of research before anyone can be confident of proposing ways to ensure their survival. Success is measured by the degree to which animals that are released back into the wild adapt back to their native habitat and survive as the basis for a regenerated population.

Jersey Zoo aims to educate visitors, too. That is what makes a visit to Jersey Zoo so fascinating – there is far more to see and do than merely to stare at the animals. A visitor

Ring-tailed lemur.

centre, with video presentations, explains the philosophy
and work of the Jersey Wildlife
Preservation Trust. Throughout the day there are talks and
activities, and you can handle
a python or learn about
lowland gorillas with the help
of knowledgeable and dedicated keepers. Information
boards explain what is known
about the animals, which
include fruit bats and orang-
utans, spectacled bears and
lemurs, aye-ayes and tamarins,
Chilean flamingoes and the
St Lucia parrot – an eclectic
mix united by one common
characteristic: they are all very
close to disappearing
altogether from the wild, and
would very soon be extinct,
but for the safety net provided
by Jersey Zoo.

Lowlands gorilla.

GUERNSEY ★

St Peter Port ★★

Guernsey's capital, St Peter Port, owes its
attractiveness to the fact that it sits on the
edge of a very steep escarpment, which
drops some 61m (200ft) from the heights of
the lovely Candie Gardens down to sea level.
Built on a series of terraces, the town
tumbles down the steep hillside, its
appealing mixture of granite warehouses
and pastel-painted houses linked by tiny
cobbled alleys, too narrow for cars to
penetrate. Among this maze of little lanes
there are many graceful Regency houses that
would not look out of place in Cheltenham,
Tunbridge Wells or Bath, and many good
shops, with their original shop-fronts intact.

A good place to start exploring is the
Guernsey Information Centre on the North
Esplanade, a grand building designed in
1911 as the base for the island's
government, and now the place to go for
books, leaflets and maps about the islands of
Guernsey Bailiwick. Westwards along the
Quay, the marinas and piers to the left are
busy with the comings and goings of inter-
island ferry craft, fishing boats, luxury yachts
and high-speed catamarans linking
Guernsey to ports in England and France.
To the right, tall granite warehouses, once
filled with exotic imports from the
Mediterranean and the Caribbean, have
now been converted to cafés, shops and
pubs. In between, narrow stepped alleys,
called *venelles*, lead uphill to the High Street,
where Guernsey's excellent range of up-
market shops are to be found.

The busy road junction at the end of the
Quay has two major landmarks. To the right

Sailing yachts rest up in St Peter Port harbour.

are the **Town Church★**, or St Peter's, its beautifully traceried 15C windows filled with modern stained glass, and the statue of Prince Albert, commemorating a visit made by Victoria and Albert in 1846.

Beyond lies Castle Pier, giving access to Castle Cornet and to the lighthouse from which there are fine backwards **views** from the harbour to St Peter Port. **Castle Cornet★** explodes daily to the sound of the noonday gun, set off by two soldiers in 18C uniform, and it is worth being here for the event if you can. The maze of buildings and gardens within the angular ramparts include the

earliest Elizabethan fortifications, Napoleonic extensions and Second World War bunkers. The 18C barracks contain two excellent museums: one details the history of the castle using realistic tableaux, while the **Maritime Museum** has a reconstruction of the Gallo-Roman boat excavated in St Peter Port, along with items from its cargo. Above the Maritime Museum is an art gallery full of portraits of Guernsey notables and dramatic 18C seascapes, and housed in the Hospital Building is the **Militia Museum**, devoted to the history of the Royal Guernsey militia.

Evening falls on Castle Cornet, St Peter Port, as the Condor ferry comes into harbour.

From the Castle Pier, turning left will take you along South Esplanade to the town's main bathing beaches, which are backed by high cliffs and attractive public gardens. Tunnelling into the cliffs are two attractions. **La Valette Underground Military Museum** is housed in a series of tunnels built by prisoner-of-war labour during the Occupation as a refuelling station for U-boats. One of the huge oil tankers used to store fuel has survived, and well-mounted displays tell the fascinating human story behind what was to prove the most traumatic period in the islands' history, using contemporary diaries, letters, photographs and newspapers. Food was commandeered, and the islanders lived on a near-starvation diet; the exhibits here include the contents of food parcels delivered by the Swedish Red Cross ship, the *Vega*, providing relief from survival rations that included parsnip coffee, seaweed jelly and blackberry-leaf tea.

Nearby, the **Aquarium** is housed in another tunnel – this time constructed in the 19C as part of a scheme, never completed, to drive a road through to the adjoining bay. Displayed in tanks around the dark tunnels are fish from local waters, including tiny but perfectly camouflaged baby soles and the small inhabitants of rocky tide pools, plus many colourful fish from tropical waters.

The area to the north of the Castle Pier has many attractive Regency houses, and is well worth exploring if you are interested in fine architecture. At 26 Cornet Street is the fascinating **18C shop**, The Victorian Shop and Parlour, complete with its original

Georgian shutters, restored by the National Trust for Guernsey and staffed by costumed shop assistants (open April to mid-Oct, Tues, Wed, Thur, Sat 10am-4pm; 28 Nov-19 Dec for Christmas shop). Further uphill are the grand houses of Hauteville, where you can visit Victor Hugo's home, **Hauteville House★** (*see* p.68). Further north, Trinity Square is the focal point for antique shops, which spread along Mansell Street and Mill Street, leading back to Market Square, with its two covered **markets** – one for fish and meat (built in 1822) and the other for fruit and vegetables. If the latter looks considerably grander than you would expect for a humble market, it is because the town's Assembly Rooms and the income tax offices were all incorporated into the elegant ensemble when it was built in the 1780s.

From the Market Square, the High Street leads eastwards, and its many up-market boutiques, French-style bistros and well-

Enter the private world of a literary giant and man of genius.

Medals and wartime paraphernalia are displayed in tunnels built by prisoners of war in La Valette Underground Military Museum.

stocked bookshops will delay your progress as you window-shop or stop for a coffee. Wide Smith Street leads left and on uphill to the imposing **Royal Court House**, seat of justice on the island, and on, via Anne Street, up to one of St Peter Port's busiest roads. Cross over to Candie Road and the peace of flower-filled **Candie Gardens**, with their panoramic views and statue of Victor Hugo. The pretty French-style bandstand has now been turned into a café, and the modern building alongside houses the **Guernsey Museum and Art Gallery**, where the displays chart Guernsey's history, from prehistoric times to the present day. Children can try completing the quiz as parents learn about the highly productive glasshouses, which were the basis of the island's horticulture from the mid-19C, or admire the paintings on display.

Colourful flags and bunting deck out St Peter Port's busy High Street.

Victor Hugo

Today we would regard Victor Hugo (1802-85) as a harmless eccentric, whose beliefs could easily be put down to the artistic temperament. In mid-19C France, he was branded a dangerous radical, and sent into exile for his opposition to the *coup d'état* staged by Prince Louis Napoléon in 1851.

Hugo chose Jersey as his new home because he could not speak English and because he wanted to remain within sight of the shores of his native land. He brought his mistress (Juliette Drouet) with him, as well as his wife and family, referring to one as 'Madame, la mère de mes enfants' and the other as 'Madame, mon amie'.

Hugo kept up a tirade of invective against 'Napoléon le petit', as he styled the French Emperor, and his newspaper, *L'Homme*, fiercely criticised Queen Victoria for making a state visit to Paris in 1855. This so angered the people of Jersey that Hugo was expelled once again, and, after contemplating exile in Belgium, decided to move to Guernsey instead.

Not long after arriving on the island, he began to receive significant royalties from two recently published volumes of poems and he was able, for the first time in his life, to buy a house, rather than renting. He purchased **Hauteville House★** at a knock-down price because the previous owner had committed suicide, and nobody else was keen to live there, despite its size and grandeur, its magnificent views and its large garden.

While living at Hauteville House, Hugo not only wrote some of his best-remembered novels (including *Les Misérables*), but also discovered a love for interior decoration, and the house as it survives today is entirely his creation. It is a strange and eccentric house, reflecting many of Hugo's wilder ideas and passions. Walls and ceilings are lined with heavy Aubusson tapestries, and several rooms have dark panelling and fireplaces built from antique

Victor Hugo strides out in the grounds of the Guernsey Museum and Art Gallery.

wooden chests and church pews. On the top floor he created an eyrie of glass from which to look out over the islands of Sark and Herm to his beloved France, which honoured him with a state funeral and burial in the Panthéon after his death in 1885 (closed Oct to April).

Southern Guernsey

Guernsey divides naturally into two distinct halves. In the southern 'highland' region, the coast is fringed by rocky cliffs and tiny sheltered bays that are difficult to get to but worth seeking out for privacy and scenic value. **Fermain Bay**, immediately south of St Peter Port, is a perfect example. There is no road access and no nearby parking; instead, the beach is reached along a lovely path that passes through woodland fringed by flowery banks and full of bluebells in late spring. Easier to reach is **Jerbourg Point★**, further south, with road access down to a headland with plenty of parking, and sweeping **views** of Guernsey's island neighbours.

La Gran'mère du Chimquière, the Grandmother of the Cemetery, is said to guarantee fertility.

Trees and a Napoleonic pepperpot tower back the charming quiet beach of Fermain Bay.

To reach Jerbourg Point, you will pass the entrance to **Sausmarez Manor**, an elegant Queen Anne house dating from 1714, which offers a range of attractions. You can wander in the rambling semi-tropical gardens that surround the imposing house, scattering free-range ducks and hens as you go, or you can take advantage of the nine-hole pitch-and-putt course alongside. For children the miniature steam railway is a big adventure, and there is a fascinating dolls' house collection to admire. Best of all are the guided tours of the house, which reveal much about the island, and the role played by one of Guernsey's oldest and most distinguished families in its history.

Just round the corner from the manor, pretty **St Martin's Church** is found at the end of a maze of narrow lanes. Standing by the gate is the formidable **Gran'mère du**

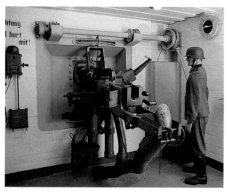

Everything from machine-guns to food parcels and personal momentos are displayed in the German Occupation Museum.

Just the spot to sit and take in the splendid coastal views, at Icart Point.

Chimquière★, a carved granite figure which was already more than 2 000 years old when the Romans arrived in Guernsey. Originally carved some time between 2500 and 1800 BC, this mother goddess was given breasts, folded arms and a girdle. During late Roman times (around AD 200 to 300) she was embellished and given facial features, a head of curls and a short buttoned cape carved on her upper torso. The statue still attracts offerings of coins and flowers, especially after a wedding in the church.

Continuing westwards along the airport road, look for a sign to the **Moulin Huet Pottery** on the left (*see* p.107). A narrow road passes the little pottery, where you can watch porcelain and stoneware vessels being made, and continues down a delightful green valley, with a bubbling stream running alongside the road, to a car park. From here, as you walk down a path to the delightful **Moulin Huet Bay** with its rock-pools, cliffs and caves, you will understand why Renoir came here on several occasions in 1883 and painted no fewer than 15 pictures of the scenic cove. The headland at **Icart Point★★** is the highest and most southerly part of the island, and commands far-reaching **views** along the coastline.

Back on the main road, the **German Occupation Museum** is signposted just before the entrance to the airport. The museum is unflinching in its account of the Occupation, and does not avoid subjects – such as black marketeering and collaboration – still painful to those islanders who lived through the war. Even so, there is much here that children and adults will find fascinating, from the letters from the Controlling Committee for the

States of Guernsey giving details on the distribution of food and arrangements for the slaughtering of pigs, to the recipes for potato cake, marrow pudding, seaweed jelly and blackberry-leaf tea. There is a reconstruction of an 'Occupation Kitchen', and of shops, houses and cafés in St Peter Port as they looked during the war. The museum tea-room offers such delicacies as parsnip coffee, for those who want to recapture the authentic taste of the war.

Continuing west, turn left at the next junction to reach the south-western extremities of the island, where numerous bunkers and wartime relics survive, including the impressive and sculptural **Pleinmont Tower**, commanding extensive **views** of the coast. An older fortification stands on a rocky islet further north.

Travelling north, the wide **Rocquaine Bay★** opens up on the left, with its mixture of sand (at low tide) and rock-pools, a

The wide sweep of Rocquaine Bay, with Fort Grey – affectionately known as the 'cup and saucer'.

popular spot with windsurfers. In the centre of the bay, **Fort Grey** was built as part of a chain of gun emplacements designed to deter Napoleon from invading the island. The two-storey tower at the centre of the fort now forms the **Shipwreck Museum** dedicated to the island's maritime history, with finds from 18C-20C wrecks, many of which foundered on the treacherous rocks at the island's western end.

At the northern tip of Roquaine Bay is **Lihou Island**. If the tide is out, you can cross the causeway and visit the ruins of the 12C Benedictine **Priory of St Mary**. The same headland has a number of Neolithic passage graves, or dolmens. Below the headland known as Fort Saumarez, dominated now by a German tower, is the **Creux ès Faies**

Crossing the causeway to Lihou Island.

dolmen ('Entrance to Fairyland'), with its intact mound and dating from 2000-1800 BC. A short way north, **Le Trépied** has massive capstones and was, according to local tradition, where local witches once gathered for their revels.

If you continue along the coast road, and then take the next left turn, you will come to the island's oldest surviving church, the tiny **St Apolline's Chapel★**. Built in 1392 and beautifully restored in 1980, the simple building, with its granite vault, has a well-preserved medieval **fresco** of the Last Supper. Continuing inland, look for a turning right signposted to St Saviour, which winds up through a green valley, now dammed to create a reservoir, to the village centre, with its landmark church and spire. Alongside the church you will find the entrance to **St Saviour's Tunnels**, an underground storage depot dug into the hillside beneath the church during the Occupation. The Germans used the tunnels as an ammunition store in the belief that the British were unlikely to bomb the church. Only a short stretch of tunnel is now open, because of a long-running dispute between the various owners, and the displays consist largely of military equipment left in the tunnel at the end of the Occupation.

Just south of the parish, **The Hanging Strawberry Farm** is exactly that – polythene tunnels where strawberry plants are

Creating something a little different, at Guernsey Woodcarvers.

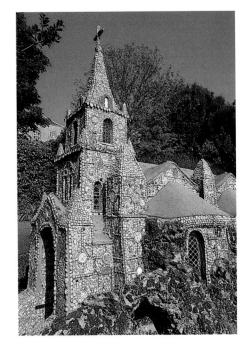

The Little Chapel is a model of the grotto and shrine at Lourdes, created from shells and pottery fragments.

encouraged to produce a prolific crop, planted in grow-bags suspended in mid-air and fed by water-born nutrients. Other attractions include a crazy-golf course, café and shop, and the **Guernsey Woodcarvers** workshop, where you can watch antiques being restored and the production of a variety of lathe-turned objects.

Several more attractions can be found in the immediate vicinity. The quirky **Little Chapel★**, built almost entirely from pottery and shells by French monks in the 1920s, has a place in the record books for being one of the world's smallest churches. **Guernsey**

Bird Gardens has a range of birds, from parrots to penguins, in aviaries set around flower-filled gardens, plus a jungle play area for children. At **Guernsey Clockmakers**, you can admire the intricate craftsmanship involved in making clocks and barometers. Returning to the theme of war, the **German Underground Military Hospital** (west of St Peter Port) is a reminder that Hitler fully expected the British to try and recapture the Channel Islands, which is why Guernsey and its neighbours were so heavily fortified. Any casualties resulting from the attempt to breach the Atlantic Wall defences would have been brought here for treatment, though, in the event, the tunnels were only ever used for storage.

Northern Guernsey

Northern, or 'lowland', Guernsey has fewer formal attractions than the south of the island, but it makes up for this in the number of fine sandy beaches fringing the west-facing coast. If you are heading this way, be sure to bring swimming costumes and towels, so you can take advantage of the sun and sand. **Côbo Bay★★**, with its striking red rocks and sandy shore, is ideal for surfing, swimming and rock-pooling, while to the south is the wide, sandy beach of **Vazon Bay**.

Heading westwards out of St Peter Port, enjoy a drive along the scenic and steep sided Talbot Valley, which descends from the plateau of northern Guernsey, past tiny cow-filled fields, to the flatter and more densely populated south. Marking the northernmost end of the valley is the **Brooklands Farm Implements Museum**, with displays of tools and machinery used on the island over the last 100 years.

Much the same ground is covered at the excellent **Guernsey Folk Museum★**, in the grounds of **Saumarez Park★**, further east. Children are very well catered for here, with a modern adventure playground (suitable for children up to eight years old) and a friendly tearoom with a disco and play area. The big French-style manor house at the centre of the estate is now a home for the elderly, but the ground-floor rooms are open to the public, and the gardens are full of semi-tropical trees and shrubs. The Battle of Flowers is held here every year (fourth Thursday in August). The Folk Museum, run by the National Trust of Guernsey, is set in the farm buildings to the rear, and has displays on domestic and working life in Guernsey at the turn of the century.

Pleasant gardens and converted farm buildings make an attractive setting for the Oatlands Craft Centre.

At the nearby **Telephone Museum**, nostalgia and social history combine in the story of telecommunications on the island since the formation of the States Telephone Council in 1896 – and children are allowed to touch and play with many of the phones on display (closed Oct-April). Even so, they will probably prefer the colour and grace of the free-flying butterflies on display at **Le Friquet: the Centre of Attractions**, or the radio-controlled cars, the mini-golf and croquet and the Activity World play area.

A mile or so further north is the location of the **Guernsey Freesia Centre**, with its colourful blooms and sweetly scented polythene tunnels. Videos explain the impressive growth of the cut-flower industry on Guernsey, which sends millions of blooms to the UK every year. The nearby **Oatlands Craft Centre** occupies a converted brickworks, with converted sheds grouped among the disused bottle kilns to provide premises for a chocolate maker, jeweller, pottery, glass-blower, Christmas Barn and Guernsey Woollens outlet.

Immediately north is **Ladies Bay**, one of Guernsey's many tempting beaches, with soft pink-white sand interspersed by granite outcrops, sculpted by the wind. Every headland along this northern coast has its fortress and dolmen – indeed, at a certain spot along the north-coast road alongside **L'Ancresse Common**, the horizon bristles with tall circular towers from the Napoleonic era. Much of the common is used as a golf course, but hidden among the gorse is the island's oldest prehistoric structure, the roofless burial chamber called **Les Fouaillages**, discovered as recently as 1977 yet constructed over 7 000 years ago. Even more impressive is **Le Déhus**, tucked down a rural lane off the main road as it turns south back towards Bordeaux Harbour. More than any passage grave on the island, Le Déhus retains its ancient sense of mystery. One of the capstones has a carving in relief of a bearded man known as Le Gardien du Tombeau – dramatically spotlit, the carved figure pre-dates the tomb, which itself is more than 4 000 years old.

Returning south to St Peter Port, you will pass the fishing port at **Bordeaux Harbour** and then the busy **St Sampson**, with its shipyards and commercial docks. Expanded when the island was exporting huge quantities of granite for paving and road construction to the UK, Guernsey's second port is still busy with vessels carrying oil and coal for the power station, as well as timber and grain.

The haunting prehistoric burial chamber of Le Déhus is one of the islands' best preserved.

81

HERM

Herm is Guernsey's nearest neighbour, and is easily reached by fast ferries that depart from St Peter Port every hour during the day, docking at the harbour at high tide and at the landing steps of Rosière at low tide. The 20 minutes that it takes to cross to Herm is time in which to prepare for the island's unspoiled and other-worldly atmosphere. Herm is completely free of cars, and the hills and hidden hollows are bright with meadow flowers and butterflies. With no cars to worry about, families can enjoy the freedom to explore the island, and anyone with children should head straight for the wonderful **Shell Beach**, at the island's north-eastern tip, a 15-minute walk from the ferry port. Here, thanks to tidal action and the warm Gulf Stream, the beach has been formed out of countless millions of shells and shell fragments – a beachcomber's dream.

If you are feeling energetic and want to see the whole of the island, you can walk all the way round the coast, heading north towards Oyster Rock, past an almost continuous sweep of firm sand and dune. The **Pierre aux Rats**, at the island's northern tip, is a modern obelisk marking the point where, for thousands of years, a huge granite stone had stood, erected in prehistoric times and demolished by 19C quarrymen looking for building stone.

Map of Herm

Rounding Shell Beach, with its café, the path continues past the viewpoint at **Le Grand Monceau★** to the sheltered **Belvoir Bay**, another good place to bathe. Continue all the way south and you will have a good view from the clifftops at **Sauzebourge Point** of **Jethou**, the 40ha (100 acre) private island that was once the home of Compton Mackenzie (his book, *Fairy Gold*, is set on Herm and Jethou).

Herm's special character is the result of the hard work of Peter Wood, who was the Tenant until his death in 1998, and whose family continue to lease the island from the States of Guernsey. When the Wood family took on the lease in 1949, they arrived to find the island so overgrown that it took three weeks to find the house that is now their home. The story of how they

Collecting is certainly compulsive, on Herm's Shell Beach.

83

transformed the island into a semi-tropical paradise over the next 30 years is told in a delightful book entitled *Herm, our Island Home*, written by the late Jenny Wood. The Wood's family residence, the 15C **Manor**, is the main building at the centre of the island, where it forms a settlement known as **Le Manoir Village**, with the island's power station, dairy farm, and some self-catering cottages. The little church nearby, **St Tugual's Chape**l, dates from the 11C and has some striking stained-glass windows, as well as a memorial in the adjacent garden dedicated to Jenny Wood, who died in 1991.

Refreshments and shopping are catered for at the harbour, where The White House, the island's only hotel, has an up-market restaurant serving delicious seafood, including local Herm oysters. Less formal alternatives include the Ship Inn and the Mermaid Tavern, both offering a choice of bar snacks and full restaurant meals.

It's easy to find your way round the small island of Herm.

SARK★★

An enchanted island where the noise and bustle of the 20C are soon forgotten.

Sark consists of a flat-topped volcanic plateau, rising to 110m (360ft) above sea level, fringed by steep cliffs. Nowhere is the island's make-up more dramatically experienced than at the narrow and vertiginous isthmus, called La Coupée, which connects the two parts of the island, the northerly Great Sark and the southerly Little Sark. For many visitors, the experience of driving across La Coupée in a horse-drawn cart, is the highlight of a visit to the

Map of Sark

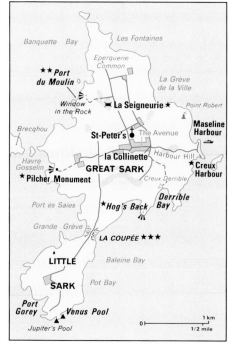

island, but there are plenty of other attractions, so the five hours that you will have on the island, between ferry journeys from St Peter Port, will pass very rapidly. Cars are prohibited on the island, but bicycles can be hired to speed you around the lanes if you want to get the most from a visit, though for most visitors it is the relaxed and gentle pace of life that gives Sark its special appeal.

Ferries from St Peter Port depart daily at 8am and 10am, and take 45 minutes to cross to the jetty on the eastern side of the island, docking at Maseline Harbour. Opposite is **Creux Harbour★**, the picturesque original harbour which is dry at low tide. It is a stiff climb up Harbour Hill for half a mile to the village of **La Collinette**, at the centre of the island (visitors arriving with luggage or needing a lift are met by one of the island's

Creux Harbour is linked to the village by a tunnel, seen in the centre here, and a steep climb up the hill.

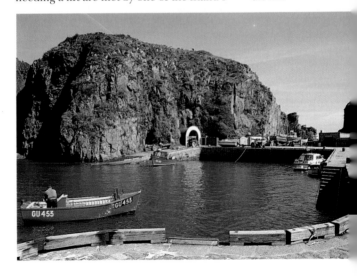

The less energetic can opt for an easier way to see the sights.

unique tractor-drawn buses). Some people do not make it as far as the village – arriving at the harbour, you may be tempted by the offer of a boat trip around the island, which is an ideal way to see the towering cliffs, with their nesting seabirds, and to enter otherwise inaccessible sea caves. You can also opt for an excursion of an hour or two's duration by horse-drawn cart, which will meet you at the top of Harbour Hill and take you off to see the sights in old-fashioned comfort.

Walking up through the village, you can compare menus at the hotels and pubs along the way, and make a mental note to return for lunch. Note, too, the **Prison**, a cramped two-cell gaol, built in Napoleonic times, but still used to hold law-breakers before packing them off to Guernsey for trial.

Sark's wartime experiences are

commemorated in the **Sark Occupation Museum**, which celebrates the doughty courage of the stalwart Dame Sybil Hathaway, who kept up a campaign of resistance to Nazi rule throughout the Occupation.

Dame Sybil was the hereditary ruler of Sark from 1927 until her death in 1974, glorying in the title of Le Seigneur, a title currently enjoyed by her grandson, Michael Beaumont. Head north from the village, past **St Peter's Church**, and you will come to **La Seigneurie★**, the home of Sark's ruler. The house itself is not open to the public, but you can enjoy the delightful walled gardens that surround the house, spilling over with a profusion of colourful flowers. The Seigneur not only enjoys this glorious spot, but also has considerable powers, bestowed upon his ancestors by Elizabeth I in 1563. For this reason it is often said that Sark is Europe's last feudal state, but the

The public can explore the luxuriant gardens of La Seigneurie, residence of the Seigneur of Sark.

constitution has been modified since the 16C; government is now the responsibility of elected representatives, though the Seigneur still enjoys the right to a tax of one-thirteenth of the value of any Sark property that changes hands.

This tax, known as Le Treizième, is the only significant tax that the island's 550 residents face, since there are no income taxes, death duties, capital gains taxes or customs and VAT duties to pay on the island. Among recently arrived residents wishing to take advantage of this generous regime are the super-wealthy Barclay brothers, who purchased the island of Brecqhou, just off Sark's western coast, in 1993, providing builders on the Channel Islands with a five-year bonanza while they constructed an ultra-modern hideaway on the island, disguised as a Gothic castle.

The walk across La Coupée is not for the faint-hearted.

A road to the north of La Seigneurie turns into a path leading across the clifftops to the

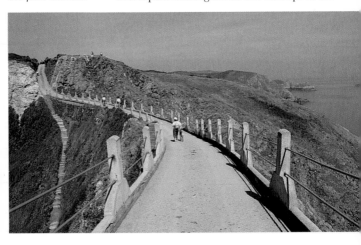

Window in the Rock, which was created in the 1850s to provide a splendid view of the **Port du Moulin★★**.

South of the village, winding lanes lead to **La Coupée★★★**, one of Sark's unmissable sights. This knife-edge ridge is topped by a road just wide enough for a horse and cart to cross, with a drop of 79m (260ft) to either side. La Coupée was once even more hazardous: narrow, crumbling and unprotected, the path across the top was widened and fenced at the end of the

Second World War. From this spot you can descend by a steep path to the sandy **Grande Grève** beach. Alternatively, continue south to explore the ruins of engine houses and chimneys, all that remains of the **silver mines** at the southern tip of Little Sark. Silver was found here in the 19C, but not in sufficient quantities to prevent the Sark Mining Company from going bankrupt in 1847.

In the rocky coves below the mines is the intriguingly named **Venus Pool**, which is worth seeking out for a dip on a hot day. This natural rock-pool is deep enough to dive into, and there are others nearby, including the Pool of Adonis further south. If you do not wish to go so far for bathing, head north from La Coupée and seek out **Dixcart Bay** (pronounced Deecart), or **Derrible Bay**, on the south coast of Great Sark, both of which have cliff-sheltered sandy beaches. Dixcart Bay has the added advantage of its proximity to the Dixcart Hotel, where non-residents can use the welcoming bars and restaurants.

ALDERNEY

Alderney is a roughly rectangular island, bordered by low cliffs to the south and a series of sheltered bays to the north. Ferries to Alderney from Guernsey take about 45 minutes, but you can also take the 15-minute flight from St Peter Port in one of the bright yellow Trislander aircraft run by the island's own airline (Aurigny – named from the island's old French name).

Ferries dock at the island's long breakwater, a 90m (3 000ft) long granite structure built in the 19C. The **railway** that

A steep climb from La Coupée will take you down to Grande Grève beach.

was built to carry granite to the breakwater from quarries in the north of the island still survives, offering visitors the incongruous sight of two former London Underground carriages, running along the tracks among the gorse-covered dunes. The station is a short walk from the breakwater, and rides take 15 minutes or so (trains only operate at weekends and on bank holidays). At the northern end you can walk to the bathing beach at **Corblets Bay**, or the **Quesnard lighthouse** (sometimes open in the afternoons), with its fine **panorama★**.

As you travel the line, you will also see some of the many fortifications that make Alderney a rich field for anyone interested in military architecture. Because Alderney occupies such a strategic position, jutting out into the Channel and commanding the sea lanes between France and England, the island has defences from every age,

Map of Alderney

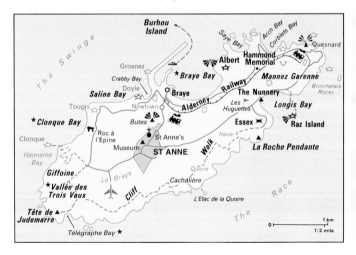

A long way from home! Today, former London underground carriages transport visitors around Alderney.

Quesnard lighthouse, with the ruined Fort Hommeaux Florains on the islet to the left.

including the remains of a Roman fort on Longis Bay. Some of the more spectacular defences, such as **Fort Albert** and **Fort Quesnard**, date from the Tudor, Napoleonic and Victorian eras. The island is especially rich in Second World War fortifications, built by the Germans after the British

authorities had evacuated the island. The
Nazis turned Alderney into a heavily defended
artillery platform, deploying prisoners of
war as forced labourers. The **Hammond
Memorial**, at the northern end of the island,
commemorates those mainly Russian, Polish
and Jewish slave labourers who met their
deaths here during that period.

Immediately opposite the main railway
station is **Braye Harbour★**, with one of
Alderney's best beaches. Here too you will
find **The Shed**, a small museum displaying
items that are being rescued by marine
archaeologists from the wreck of an
Elizabethan ship found just 800m (2 625ft)
off the island's north coast.

Southwards lies the charming capital,
St Anne, where handsome Georgian houses
and whitewashed cottages line the granite
cobbled streets, along with many welcoming

*Braye Bay, the
largest beach on
the island, offers
good bathing with
views of the
harbour.*

shops, cafés and restaurants. The Alderney Society's small **museum**, housed in the island's former school (built 1790), contains Occupation-era relics and archaeological finds, as well as photographs and pictures documenting the island's recent history.

Further south still is **Telegraph Bay★**, which, despite the proximity of the airport, is a good place for bathing at low tide. Its name derives from the Telegraph Tower (1811) which sent a repeating signal via Sark, providing communications with Jersey and Guernsey. Just offshore, Les Etacs rocks look as if they are covered in frost, but the white coating is the guano from one of southern Britain's biggest gannet colonies. Further offshore, **Burhou Island**, with its eroded rock stacks, is home to a colony of puffins (both islands can be seen at closer quarters if you join one of the island boat tours advertised in Braye and St Anne's).

Some of the offshore rocks support large colonies of gannets.

WEATHER

The Channel Islands receive more hours of sunshine than any other part of the British Isles, but the best of the weather occurs from May to October, when daytime temperatures range from 20°C to 30°C and the sun shines for an average of eight hours. Visiting the Channel Islands out of season, you may find that ferries to Sark and Herm are occasionally cancelled because of adverse weather, and rain is an ever-present threat throughout the months of November to April. Even so, the rain is very localised, and falls in short bursts, often interspersed with sunshine. Warmed by the Gulf Stream, the islands enjoy mild and frost-free winters, providing excellent conditions for walking and cycling. The relatively warm wet air in winter can cause fogs to roll in from the sea, but generally these are rapidly dispersed by the south-westerly winds.

Jersey's Battle of Flowers.

CALENDAR OF EVENTS

The Bailiwicks of Jersey and Guernsey both have a very full programme of events, mainly timed to coincide with the peak summer holiday season. Local tourist offices publish a comprehensive monthly list, which you can obtain in advance, or pick up on arrival. Here is a selection of the more important annual festivals. Precise dates vary from year to year, so check with the tourist office.

April

Guernsey Festival of Food and Wine, throughout the month, with special gourmet menus at many restaurants and hotels.

Jersey Jazz Festival, with local and international stars in a week-long jam session, starting at the end of April and continuing into May.

May

Alderney's Milk o' Punch Sunday (first Sunday), when, between noon and 2pm, local pubs dispense free punch made from milk and rum, mixed with egg, nutmeg and sugar, the drink that put hairs on the chests of 18C seafarers.

June

Jersey Good Food Festival, with wine-tastings and traditional dishes, such as Bean Crock, as well as seafood and gourmet cuisine.

Sark's Midsummer Show is a celebration of the island's flowers and garden produce, with 'best garden' competitions and special exhibits.

July

Jersey Floral Festival, when the island's horticulturalists compete to mount lavish displays on a floral theme.

Vaier Marchi, on Guernsey, is an old-time market mounted in the grounds of Saumarez Park.

St Peter Port Town Carnival includes the usual parades and summertime events.

Sark Water Carnival is a two-day extravaganza of serious and silly boat races, water processions and events in Le Creux Harbour.

August

This festive month begins with *Alderney Week*, seven days of crazy indulgence, culminating in a torchlit parade and firework display.

Next comes *Jersey's Battle of Flowers* – the high spot of the Channel Islands' festive calendar – held in mid-August. Celebrating nature's bounty, local organisations mount lavish floats decorated with real and paper flowers, which parade down Victoria Avenue to the accompaniment of marching bands. Until 1964, the parade ended in anarchy, as enthusiastic float occupants tore their creations apart and pelted the onlookers. With more and more people attending the parade (which lasts all afternoon) the risk of injury became too great and the battle element was discontinued. Instead, the parade is now repeated the following evening; this moonlit parade culminates in a spectacular firework display staged from Elizabeth Castle.

Guernsey's Battle of Flowers, held a week later than Jersey's, is not as big, but combines a colourful parade with an agricultural fair, held in the grounds of Saumarez Park.

Finally Sark, not to be outdone, hosts its own *agricultural livestock and produce show.*

September
After August's festivities, the islands settle down to more gentle celebrations, including the *Sark Horse Show*, with carriage-driving competitions, dressage and races, and Alderney's *Juggling Festival.* Guernsey mounts a *Battle of Britain* air display over St Peter Port harbour, and Jersey marks the end of the harvest season with demonstrations of *cider making* at the Hamptonne Country Life Museum.

October
The arts predominate this month, as Jersey hosts the week-long *World Music Festival* and Guernsey has its *Jazz Festival.*

Guernsey also has a *Real Ale and Cider Festival* at the beginning of the month, matched by Jersey's *CAMRA Jersey Beer Festival* a week later.

ACCOMMODATION
The tourist boards on Jersey and Guernsey both produce annual *Where to Stay* guides, detailing hotels and guest houses in every price bracket, plus self-catering options and camp sites. These list all the **hotels** that have been registered with the tourist authorities, which effectively includes most hotels, except for a handful of very grand establishments. The tourist authorities inspect the hotels and grade them according to facilities, from the best-equipped five-star hotels, many of which have gourmet-standard restaurants, to homely bed-and-breakfast establishments. Most visitors will find three-star hotels perfectly adequate; most of these have car parking for clients, en-suite facilities, and a restaurant serving breakfast, lunch-time snacks, children's high teas and evening meals. Many also have a children's games room and a small swimming pool.

For the peak summer season, it is best to book well in advance to ensure your first choice of hotel. Out of season, many hotels offer packages, with free car hire or reduced-price half-board terms for those who stay for a whole week. You can book directly with the hotel, but package tour rates are also very competitively priced.

Self-catering is a good option if you want the freedom to shop in local markets and enjoy the abundance of good local produce, rather than eating out every night. Much self-catering is based in apartments, sharing hotel-style amenities, and at hotel prices. For better terms and greater character, look out for family-run cottages in converted farm buildings.

Guernsey has plenty of choice of self-catering units, and while conventional hotel accommodation is more usual on Jersey, an increasing number of self-catering conversions have been made in recent years. The choice is more limited on the smaller islands, but Alderney and Sark offer hotels, guest houses, bed and break-fast, holiday cottages and flats.

Note that motor-homes are not permitted on the islands, and there are no **caravan** sites. **Camping** is allowed only on recognised sites.

Recommendations

Jersey
Longueville Manor
(Longueville Road, St Saviour, Jersey JE2 7SA, ☎ 01534 25501, fax 01534 31613) Renowned country house hotel with outstanding restaurant. The 35 spacious rooms have elegant furnishings, and antiques furnish the main part of the house, which dates from the 13C.

Hotel de France (St Saviour's Road, St Helier, Jersey JE1 7XP, ☎ 01534 614000) One of Jersey's more luxurious hotels, newly refurbished, but far from stuffy, with family facilities, evening entertainment, a cinema, gym, squash courts, swimming pools and health complex with regular dance and aerobics classes.

Merton Hotel (Belvedere Hill, St Saviour, Jersey JE4 9PG, ☎ 01534 24231) The winner from a family point of view, with a huge Aquadome fun pool, complete with water slide, cascades, water cannons and spas, and the Neptune Club supervising play activities, and nightly cabarets.

L'Horizon (St Brelade's Bay, Jersey JE3 8EF, ☎ 01534 43101, fax 01534 46269) Located at the centre of St Brelade's Bay, furnished in a contemporary style with luxurious sea-facing rooms and offering a range of restaurants and leisure facilities.

Château la Chaire (Rozel Valley, Jersey JE3 6AJ, ☎ **01534 863354**, fax 01534 865137) Victorian country house set in five acres of gardens in a quiet location. Individually furnished, distinctive in style and offering a good degree of period charm.

Greenhills Country Hotel (Coin Varin, Mont de l'Ecole, Jersey JE3 3EL, ☎ **01534 481042**, fax 01534 485322) A 17C stone-built house set in charming gardens, personally run, attractively furnished and located in a tranquil setting.

A selection of less expensive hotels and guesthouses:
Moorings Hotel (Gorey Pier, Gorey, Jersey JE3 6EW, ☎ **01534 853633**, fax 01534 857618) Friendly small three-star hotel on Gorey's waterfront with Mont Orgueil Castle behind. Renowned seafood restaurant.

Champ Colin (Rue du Champ Colin, Houge Bie, Jersey JE2 7UN, ☎ **01534 851877**) Guesthouse in a part-19C farmhouse, offering comfortable accommodation in a quiet country setting (non-smokers only).

La Bonne Vie (Roseville Street, St Helier, Jersey JE2 4PL, ☎ **01534 35955**, fax 01534 33357) Centrally located,

prettily decorated Victorian house.

The Glen (Vallée des Vaux, St Helier, Jersey JE2 3GB, ☎ **01534 32062**, fax 01534 880738) Victorian house in country setting, located close to St Helier with well-equipped bedrooms.

Guernsey
Jerbourg (Jerbourg Point, St Martin, Guernsey GY4 6BJ, ☎ **01481 38826**, fax 01481 328238) Smart, modern, recently-refurbished hotel offering good comforts in a pleasant location.

Idlerocks (Jerbourg Point, St Martin, Guernsey, GY4 6BJ, ☎ **01481 37711**, fax 01481 35592) Very friendly, well-run and welcoming hotel offering superb views from the dining areas.

La Cloche (Les Traudes, Guernsey GY4 6LR, ☎ **01481 35421**, fax 01481 38258) Immaculate little hotel, friendly and informal in a secluded location.

Les Piques Country Hotel (Rue des Piques, St Saviour's, Guernsey GY7 9FW, ☎ **01481 64515**, fax 01481 65857) Characterful converted farmhouse with good facilities.

St Pierre Park (Rohais, St Peter Port, Guernsey GY1 1FD, ☎ **01481 728282**, fax 01481

712041) Grande-luxe five-crown hotel, set in 18ha (45 acres) of wooded parkland, with its own nine-hole golf course, croquet lawn and health suite with indoor pool.

Moores Central Hotel (Le Pollet, St Peter Port, Guernsey GY1 1WH, ☎ 01481 724452, fax 01481 714037) Highly commended four-crown hotel set in a granite town house in St Peter Port's French quarter, with health suite and sun terrace.

Auberge du-Val (Sous L'Eglise, St Saviour's, Guernsey GY7 9FX, ☎ 01481 63862, fax 01481 64835) Affordable home comforts in this three-crown hotel, set in an idyllic green valley near St Saviour's church; meals served in the bistro are prepared from produce grown in the hotel's own gardens.

Herm

White House Hotel (Herm GY1 3HR, ☎ 01481 722159, fax 01481 710066) Enjoy sea views and spectacular sunsets from the rooms of this beachside hotel, with a good restaurant serving seafood and French and English cuisine.

Herm Island Self Catering (Herm GY1 3HR, ☎ 01481 722377) Seventeen holiday cottages owned by the Tenant of Herm and set around the island, some in the village and others on farms or by the beach, sleeping from two to eight people.

Sark

Aval du Creux (Harbour Hill, Sark GY9 0SB, ☎ 01481 832036) Set in lovely gardens, with a renowned seafood restaurant and heated swimming pool.

Dixcart Hotel (Sark, GY9 0SD, ☎ 01481 832015, fax 01481 832164) Family-run hotel based around a 16C farmhouse. Cliff paths run through woods from the hotel to the bathing beach at Dixcart Bay. Good restaurant serving fish, seafood and local free-range produce.

Alderney

Fort Clonque (details from the Landmark Trust, Shottesbrooke, Maidenhead, Berkshire SL6 3SW, ☎ 01628 825925) Man your own Victorian fortress on an island just off Alderney's west coast (linked by a tidal causeway). Built in the 1840s, Fort Clonque was rescued from dereliction by the Landmark Trust and converted to holiday accommodation, sleeping up to 11 people in the former soldiers' and officers' quarters.

FOOD AND DRINK

Eating out is a very important part of a Channel Islands holiday, with restaurants at every level, from award-winning gourmet havens, catering to the islands' many wealthy residents with adventurous and eclectic food, to humble but outstanding fish-and-chip cafés, or pubs offering a range of tempting bar snacks.

Fish and Seafood

Simply to wander round the markets in St Peter Port or St Helier will give you an idea of the wealth of fresh local ingredients available to the restaurateurs of the Channel Islands. Seafood is cheap, fresh and abundant: many pubs and cafés serve fresh crab sandwiches or lobster salads at affordable prices, along with oysters, scallops, spider crab, mussels and prawns – combine them all and you get a tempting *salade de fruits de mer*, similar to those that are so popular in neighbouring Normandy and Brittany.

One seafood dish that is now sadly rare is the ormer, or 'sea ear', once a staple of the Channel Islands diet, but now gathered almost to extinction. Related to the abalone, it is an oyster-like mollusc, found in the island's tidal sandbanks, with a taste that some compare to mushrooms, others to chicken. Ormers can still be found on the menus of such top restaurants as the Longueville Manor and the Cobo Bay Hotel (*see below*) during the ormer-gathering season, which lasts from January to the end of April on Guernsey and from September to April on Jersey.

Among fish, sea-bass is caught locally and frequently served Chinese-style – steamed with garlic, ginger and spring onions – and grilled sole is a favourite, along with brill, monkfish, mackerel and mullet, and conger eel, which is made into a delicious soup.

Vegetables

King of the vegetables on Jersey is the deliciously earthy Jersey Royal new potato. This far-from-humble potato deserves its royal epithet: steamed or boiled to waxy perfection, and served with butter and herbs, it is a dish fit for any monarch – look out for it from March onwards.

Market gardening thrives on all the islands, but the hydroponic methods used to produce early crops of strawberries, celery, courgettes, peppers and other salad ingredients do not always produce the most flavoursome products. Fortunately, some horticulturists still depend upon good, old-fashioned sun and soil, and a number of the better restaurants grow their own fresh produce. If you are self-catering, look out for home-grown produce sold by the roadside in what are known locally as 'hedge stalls', with an honesty box for your money.

Dairy Products

The delicious high-fat milk produced by Channel Islands cows finds its way into all sorts of dishes in the form of cream and butter, but is rarely made into cheese. Fortunately, good farmhouse cheeses are available – imported from France, England, Ireland and Italy and sold in the markets (on Guernsey, Giovanni's Delicatessen, on Fountain Street, also has a good selection). Fresh French baguettes, the perfect accompaniment, are also to be had from the markets, along with croissants and *pain au chocolat*.

Cakes

Afternoon tea is still taken seriously by many visitors to the Channel Islands, and scores of cafés and tea gardens offer tempting variations on the theme of cakes, scones and cream. The islands also have their own specialities: Jersey

Wonders are a kind of doughnut and Guernsey *gâche* (pronounced 'gosh') is a delicious tea bread, made with fruit and generously spread with butter. You may also come across black butter, a traditional preserve made from boiling apples, sugar, lemons, cider and liquorice until they reduce to a treacle-like consistency.

Bean Crock

Another indigenous dish, which Channel Islanders claim to be the origin of baked beans, is the Jersey Bean Crock, still to be found on many a café menu. Traditionally this was a Sunday breakfast treat, reserved for the one day in the week that did not involve an early start and

Harvesting Jersey Royal potatoes.

back-breaking work in the fields. Cooked slowly overnight in the embers of the fire, the main ingredients were pigs' trotters, cider, beans and onions, though pork is usually substituted for the trotters.

Drinks

Jersey and Guernsey both have their own breweries producing local beer, and Jersey's La Mare Vineyards produce white wines and apple brandy. Most of the drinks are imported, however, to cater for the popular duty-free market, and shops on the islands stock a very wide range of wines from France and further afield. Sadly, the Channel Islands no longer produce their own cider, but some shops sell *cidre bouché* (farmhouse cider) imported from Normandy and Brittany.

Recommendations
Jersey

Admiral Wine & Ale House (12-14 St James Street, St Helier, ☎ 01534 30095) Charming and atmospheric pub serving good-value meals.

Albert J Ramsbottom (90-92 Halkett Place, St Helier, ☎ 01534 21395) Clean and friendly restaurant serving top-quality fish and chips.

Chateau La Chaire (Rozel Bay, ☎ 01534 863354) Good-value fixed-price lunches and adventurous cooking at this smart restaurant in a charming location.

Jersey Museum Café (Jersey Museum, the Weighbridge, St Helier, ☎ 01534 58060) Smart brasserie serving adventurous pasta combinations, fresh fish and salads.

Jersey Pottery (Gorey Village, Grouville, ☎ 01534 851119) Eat formally in the vine-covered conservatory-style restaurant, serving gourmet-standard seafood (*see* p.103), or in the excellent brasserie, a self-service cafeteria serving lighter seafood salads and sandwiches.

Longueville Manor (Longueville Road, St Saviour, ☎ 01534 25501) Serious food for gourmets, with a nine-course *dégustation* menu and a whole menu devoted to vegetarian dishes, all featuring the best Channel Islands produce.

Metro (75-77 Halkett Place, St Helier, ☎ 01534 510096) Modern, stylish brasserie located in the town centre.

Old Court House Inn (St Aubin's Harbour, ☎ 01534 46433) Characterful harbourside pub and restaurant frequented by locals and tourists alike.

Sea Crest (Petit Port, St Brelade, ☎ 01534 46353) Good seafood cooked in a style that borrows from France and the Orient.

Suma's (Gorey Hill, ☎ 01534 853291) Contemporary restaurant with a pleasant terrace overlooking Mont Orgueil Castle and the harbour.

The Village Bistro (Gorey Village JE3 9EP, ☎ 01534 853429) Simple bistro-style restaurant serving some of the best food on the island; very good value for money.

Guernsey

Battens/Zoe Room (1 Fountain Street, St Peter Port, ☎ 01481 729939) Two new smart, modern, informal restaurants housed in the same building.

Belle Luce (La Fosse, Moulin Huet, ☎ 01481 38764) Fine cuisine in the old-world atmosphere of an 18C manor house.

Christie's (Le Pollet, St Peter Port, ☎ 01481 726624) Smart bistro in St Peter Port's main shopping street, serving anything from a breakfast-time coffee to a set-price lunch or full evening meal.

Cobo Bay Hotel (Cobo Bay, ☎ 01481 57102) Interesting dishes with the emphasis on seafood.

Taste of India (Sunset Cottage, L'Erée, ☎ 01481 64516) Tandoori lobster and delicious garlic-flavoured tandoori salmon.

Thai Orchid (Tower Hill, St Peter Port, ☎ 01481 710088) Fresh seafood and imported spices combine to create authentic Thai dishes, with plenty of choice for vegetarians.

Thomas de la Rue Pub (Le Pollet) Busy at lunchtimes; serves traditional dishes.

Herm

The White House (Herm, ☎ 01481 722159) With its own oyster farm, this restaurant naturally features Herm oysters, alongside Guernsey plaice and scallops and imaginative vegetarian dishes.

The Ship Inn (Herm, ☎ 01481 722159) The bar of the White House, serving snacks and more elaborate meals.

Tempting seafood on display in the Jersey Pottery restaurant.

The Mermaid (Herm, ☎ 01481 722170) Village pub atmosphere, with warming fire to eat meals by in winter and outside barbecue in summer.

Sark

Aval de Creux (Sark, ☎ 01481 832036) Fresh Herm oysters, gargantuan seafood platters, seafood pancakes and succulent crab draw locals and visitors.

Dixcart Hotel (Sark, ☎ 01481 832015) Seafood dishes and snacks in the bar, or full meals in the garden and restaurant.

La Sablonnerie (Sark, ☎ 01481 832061) Its own organic farm produces much of the food; melting lobster mousse or monkfish terrine are typical offerings. Snacks, cream teas and seafood platters are served in the gardens.

Alderney

First and Last (Braye, ☎ 01481 823162) Sea views to accompany bouillabaisse, lobster, crab or scallops.

Georgian House (Victoria Street, St Anne, ☎ 01481 822471) Order *plateau de fruits de mer* in advance, or take pot luck from the daily specials. Dine out in the peaceful garden.

Hotel Chez André (Victoria Street, St Anne, ☎ 01481 822777) Seafood specialities and vegetarian dishes.

SHOPPING

With no VAT and very low import duties, there are shopping bargains to be had in the Channel Islands, but you do need to do some homework if you intend to spend a lot of money on electronics goods or luxury items. Bear in mind that the Channel Islands are not full members of the European Union, and that goods bought here may well be liable to VAT or customs duty when you take them home. Remember, too, that the cost of freighting large items home can erode any savings you make.

Perhaps the best bargains are to be had in wines and spirits, but shop around before you buy anything, because prices do vary from one outlet to another.

Shopping Centres

On Jersey, the main shopping centre is in St Helier, with most of the big UK High Street chains represented along King Street, Queen Street, and the lanes to either side, plus local department stores, such as Voisin & Co, F Le Gallais & Sons, and A de Gruchy. Local people also go to the Quennevais Shopping Centre, in St Brelade, where the shops are under cover, and where parking can be easier.

Guernsey has many small

boutiques and up-market shops along the traffic-free High Street and Le Pollet, while Mansell Street, Mill Street and Market Street are lined with antique shops selling collectibles, engravings, furnishings and china.

What to Buy

For something typical of the islands, head for the widely advertised craft and visitor centres. These combine the pleasures of shopping with video presentations, guided trails or demonstrations, so that you can watch your purchases being made and learn about the processes involved. Typical of this approach is the excellent **Jersey Pottery**, in Gorey, where you can watch the pottery being made and hand-painted with delicate flower and leaf motifs.

In the well-stocked shop you can buy anything from a complete dinner service to piggy banks and jewellery. The shop also sells condiments, pickles, candles, dried flowers, chocolates and a good choice of half-price seconds and discontinued lines.

For one-stop craft centres, with a range of products under one roof, you can try Guernsey's **Oatlands Craft Centre**, in St Sampson, Jersey's **Fine Gems and Craft Centre**, between L'Etacq and Grosnez, or the **Craft & Shopping Village** attached to Jersey's Living Legend (admission charged).

Flowers are the Channel Islands' biggest horticultural export, as you will learn if you

Moulin Huet Pottery, St Martin's, Guernsey.

visit **Jersey Flying Flowers**, at Retreat Farm, St Lawrence, or the **Guernsey Freesia Centre**, in St Sampson. Both will sell you a bouquet on the spot, or you can have flowers air-freighted home to friends and family. Another popular horticultural attraction is Jersey's **Lavender Farm**, which sells home-made scents, lotions and lavender toiletries.

Knitwear on the Channel Islands means a classic jersey sweater, or a hardwearing guernsey, as worn by sailors, fishermen and, it is said, by Admiral Nelson. See the whole range at branches of **Le Tricoteur**, on Guernsey (the best bargains are to be had from the factory shop at Perelle Bay) and **Jersey Woollen Mills** at St Ouen.

For the children, visit **Guernsey Toys**, St Peter Port, where you can choose a teddy wearing his own personalised guernsey jumper.

The Channel Islands also boast some well-known gold- and silversmiths, and there are plenty of jewellery shops to choose from. **Guernsey Pearl** (shops in St Peter Port and Guernsey Coppercraft Centre, Rocquaine Bay) offer simulated freshwater and cultivated pearls. You can even buy your own oyster and have the pearl within set in a ring or pendant while you wait.

ENTERTAINMENT AND NIGHTLIFE

Most nightlife centres on the two capitals of St Helier, Jersey, and St Peter Port, Guernsey. To find out what is going on, buy the local newspaper, or pick up the monthly *Diary of Events* from the tourist offices. Most entertainment revolves around music pubs, bars and clubs, such as **Chambers** and the **Blue Note Bar** in St Helier, or the **Golden Monkey**, on Le Pollet, and the **Buzz Bar**, Berthelot Street, St Peter Port.

The **Fort Regent Leisure Centre** (Jersey) has a theatre where classical and pop music concerts are mounted, and the Beau Séjour Leisure Centre (Guernsey) has a theatre and a two-screen cinema. **Jersey Arts Centre** (box office ☎ 01534 873767) has a full programme of classical music, dance, theatre and exhibitions, as does **St James** (a church converted to an arts centre) on Guernsey (box office ☎ 01481 711361).

SPORTS

Both Jersey and Guernsey offer a wide range of sporting opportunities, from abseiling to wreck diving. A complete A to Z, listing venues, club contacts and facilities, can be obtained from the tourist authorities – ask for the *Directory of Sport*,

Leisure and Recreation.

With so many glorious beaches to choose from, sea bathing and watersports are uppermost in the minds of most visitors, but if rainy days spoil the fun, head for one of the islands' big leisure centres: St Helier's Fort Regent, and St Peter Port's Beau Séjour Centre provide swimming pools, tennis and squash courts, playgrounds and organised activities.

Sea anglers are attracted by the rich marine life and the variety of fish regularly caught in local waters (over 70 species). Boat fishing trips are available from the harbours, or contact the local tourist office.

Shore fishing is also excellent, particularly off Alderney.

The islands' mild climate and varied habitats result in a rich plant and animal life, making them a haven for naturalists and botanists. The migratory birds which stop-over during spring and autumn, and the proliferation of seabirds, attract birdwatchers, while the numerous footpaths, Green Lanes and delightful walks which lead through wooded valleys, along dramatic cliff-tops or through dunes are ideal for walking, cycling and horse-riding.

Waterskiing off the coast of Jersey.

THE BASICS

Before You Go

Visitors arriving in the Channel Islands from other parts of the United Kingdom, and from the Republic of Ireland, do not need a passport (though you should bring one if you intend to go on a day trip to France). Other visitors need only a passport to enter the Channel Islands – no visas are required.

Getting There

Getting to the Channel Islands from the UK, Ireland and Northern France is very easy, but from other countries there are fewer direct flights or ferries, and it is easiest to travel via the UK.

By Ferry

Fast ferry services are provided by **Condor Ferries**, using modern high-speed jetfoils and catamarans. These operate between 1 April and 31 October, with various options connecting Poole or Weymouth, in Dorset, to St Malo, in Brittany, via Guernsey and Jersey. Travelling at a speed of 40 knots, the Poole to Guernsey journey takes as little as 2½ hours, while it takes around 3½ hours to Jersey. The conventional ferries take 7¾ hours to Jersey and 5 hours to Guernsey.

For further information ☎ **01305 761551**. (For travel between the islands, *see* **Excursions** p.121.)

By Air

Direct flights to Jersey and Guernsey are available from most regional airports in the UK and from Dublin, operated by:
British Airways
(☎ **0345 222111**)
Air UK
(☎ **0990 074074**)
British Midland
(☎ **0345 554554**)
Jersey European
(☎ **0990 676 676**).
In addition, Alderney has its own airline, **Aurigny Air Services**, providing flights

between Southampton, Alderney, Guernsey, Jersey, Dinard and Caen. Contact: ☎ **01481 822886** (Jersey) ☎ **01481 723474** (Guernsey).

Package deals are available through travel agents and through tour operators specialising in the Channel Islands, including Thomas Cook Holidays (☎ **01733 418300**) and the Channel Islands Travel Service (☎ **01481 35471**). Packages usually include flight and hotel bookings plus car hire, making this the most economical way to arrange your stay. Many packages offer free car hire to visitors staying seven or more nights on half-board terms (taking breakfast and the evening meal at the hotel), but car hire is, in any case, very cheap on the islands.

Calm waters at La Roque, Jersey.

A-Z

Accidents and Breakdowns

Car rental companies all have their own arrangements for accidents and breakdowns, and you will be informed of these when you collect your hire car. If you bring your own car to the Channel Islands, fully comprehensive insurance is advisable and you must, in any case, carry a valid Certificate of Insurance or International Green Card.

Check with your insurance company on the procedures to be observed in the event of an accident. Accidents involving personal injury or serious damage must be reported to the police within 24 hours. In an emergency ☎ 999 for police, fire, ambulance or coastal rescue services.

Members of the AA and RAC can use the same national callout telephone numbers as the rest of Britain:
RAC ☎ 0800 828282;
AA ☎ 0800 887766.

Accommodation see p.98

Airports

The modern airport on Jersey has good facilities for shopping and eating (there is a small branch of Marks & Spencer, selling popular clothing lines, plus a bookshop and duty-free outlet); Guernsey and Alderney have smaller airports with cafés, newsagents and duty-free shops selling a more restricted range of products.

Babysitters

Some hotels provide this service at peak holiday times (Easter and July and August). Ask for details at the time you make your booking.

Banks

Offshore banking is a major feature of the economies of the Channel Islands, and all the major UK banks and building societies have branch offices in St Helier and St Peter Port. Banks are generally open Mon-Fri, 9.30am-4.30pm, and 9.30am-12.30pm on Saturday.

Sterling is accepted on all

the Channel Islands, so UK visitors do not need to change any money. You can also use UK cheques (backed by a cheque guarantee card), travellers' cheques (with a passport as identification), credit cards or cash machine cards (with a PIN number). The Bailiwicks of Guernsey and Jersey issue their own banknotes and coins, and these can be used only in the respective Bailiwick (Jersey currency is not legal tender, for example, in the UK or in Guernsey, though banks will accept notes and exchange them for sterling or Guernsey money). Many banks have two cash dispensers (ATMs): one issues sterling and the other issues local currency. Most hotels and restaurants will accept travellers' cheques, Eurocheques or the main credit cards.

Bicycles

Cycling is fun and greatly encouraged on the Channel Islands, with bikes widely available for hire and a network of 'Green Lanes' where cyclists and walkers have priority over motor vehicles. A great deal of investment has been made in developing waymarked routes for cyclists. Guides to these, along with maps and guides for cyclists, are available from many bookshops and from the Jersey and Guernsey Visitor Centres (*see* **Tourist Information**).

On Jersey, the following companies offer bike hire and guided group rides in the company of an expert guide: Jersey Cycletours ☎ 01534 482898; Zebra Cycles and Tours ☎ 01534 36556.

On Guernsey cycles can be hired from Elite Cycle Hire ☎ 01481 58518; Quay Cycle Hire ☎ 01481 714146.

On Alderney contact Puffin Cycle Hire, ☎ 01481 823725.

On Sark contact Avenue Cycle Hire ☎ 01481 832102.

Books

Classics set in the Channel islands include Compton Mackenzie's *Fairy Gold* and Victor Hugo's portrait of Jersey life, *Toilers of the Sea*. Among non-fiction, John Nettles has written several well-illustrated guides to Jersey's history and traditions, while G B Edwards' *The Book of Ebenezer Le Page* describes Guernsey. Jenny Wood's memoir, *Herm, Our Island Home*, tells how she and her husband transformed the island of Herm from a bramble-infested rock into a semi-tropical paradise. Island bookshops are well stocked with accounts of the Occupation period, from personal reminiscences to technical descriptions of the island fortifications.

Breakdowns see **Accidents**

Buses see **Transport**

Camping
Caravans and motor homes are not permitted in the Channel Islands, but campers are welcome, and there are designated sites on Jersey, Guernsey, Alderney and Herm, with fully equipped tents for hire as well as space for private campers. For details contact the Jersey and Guernsey Tourist Boards (*see* **Tourist Information**) and ask for their free *Where to Stay* booklets.

Car hire
Because there is no VAT or import duty, car hire in the Channel Islands is among the cheapest in the world, as is petrol. Cars can be collected from the harbour or airport on arrival, or delivered to your

Corbière Lighthouse, Jersey.

hotel. Hirers must be at least 20 years old, having held a full licence for at least a year. Cars cannot be hired by anyone with endorsements for dangerous or drunken driving within the last five years.

The big international firms are all represented locally, and can be booked in advance of your arrival, along with several Channel Islands firms, including Falles Hire Cars in Jersey (☎ 01534 43222), Harlequin Hire Cars in Guernsey (☎ 01481 39511) and Alderney Hire Cars on Alderney (☎ 01481 832352).

Cars are delivered to you with a quarter-full tank of petrol and you are expected to return it empty. A quarter of a tank will take you a long way on the islands, but do not worry if you just want to top up with a gallon or two – garages are quite used to this. Hire cars are also prominently marked with a large letter H, which serves as a useful warning to local drivers that you may not be familiar with the island's extremely narrow roads and difficult junctions.
See also **Driving**

Children

Perfect for children, the Channel Islands offer sheltered bathing, rock-pools to explore, boat trips to traffic-free islands, and a range of attractions, including zoos, castles, butterfly centres, shipwreck museums and underground war museums.

The castles and museums run by the Jersey and Guernsey Museums Services (*see* pp.20 and 21) make a special effort to involve children, with excellent quiz sheets and special events throughout the school holidays. Actors dressed in period costume bring to life the highly disciplined regime of soldiers garrisoned in Elizabeth Castle or Castle Cornet in the 18C, and the costumed staff at Hamptonne Country Life Museum lead children through the daily farm routine in the 17C, from bread making to milking.

For rainy days, Fort Regent, on Jersey, and the Beau Séjour Centre, on Guernsey, offer swimming pools, adventure playgrounds, cinema and café all under one roof. Better still, if you stay in the Merton Hotel, on Jersey (*see* p.99), your children get free unlimited use of the attached Aquadome fun pool, with its water slides and cascades (there are also supervised play activities, so that parents can have an hour or two each day on their own).

Many hotels serve children's

high tea (usually around 5.30pm), and children are generally made to feel special in most hotels and restaurants, where high chairs will be provided and lively behaviour is generally tolerated.

Churches see **Religion**

Climate see **p.96**

Clothing
Most visitors to the Channel Islands are on holiday, so clothing etiquette tends to be relaxed and informal. Except in the grandest hotels and restaurants, you will not be expected to dress for dinner. On the other hand, you can expect curt service if you walk into a shop or café in beach-wear or minus a shirt. Topless bathing is fine so long as it is not flaunted, and nobody minds nude bathing if you choose a private and unfre-quented beach.

Clothes are sold according to UK sizes, though most stores now give UK and European sizes on their labels. Many UK clothing chains have shops in

Pretty springtime cottages, Le Variouf Cottages, Guernsey.

St Helier and St Peter Port, including Marks & Spencer, selling clothes at around 10 per cent less than they would cost in the UK.

Consulates
Since the Channel Islands delegate foreign affairs to the UK government, there are no embassies or consulates on the islands.

Crime
As you will learn if you watch the local TV station, petty crime in the Channel Islands rarely rises above the level of the occasional drink-induced acts of vandalism (often committed by visitors rather than locals), and there is little serious crime. Nevertheless, the holiday season offers opportunities for pickpockets and thieves, and while you are unlikely to be the victim of any crime it is just as well to be vigilant and take sensible precautions.
• Carry as little money and as few credit cards as possible, and leave any valuables in the hotel safe.
• Carry wallets and purses in secure pockets inside your outer clothing, wear body belts, or carry handbags across your body or firmly under your arm.

• Cars, particularly hire cars, can be a target for opportunists, so never leave your car unlocked, and hide away or, better still, remove items of value.
• Ask your hotel for help in the first instance if you lose anything, or contact the nearest police station. If your passport is lost or stolen, report it to the police at once.

Currency see Money

Customs and Entry Regulations
The Channel Islands are associate members of the European Union (EU), rather than full members, so the customs allowances are the same as for non-EU countries:

Cigarettes	200 or
Cigarillos	100 or
Cigars	50 or
Tobacco	250 gms
Still table wine	2 litres
Spirits (22% or more)	1 litre or
Fortified/Sparkling Wine	2 litres or
An additional still table wine allowance of	2 litres
Perfume	60cc
Toilet water	250cc
Personal allowance for other goods	£145

Allowances for tobacco and alcohol apply only to people over 17 years of age, and the personal allowances cannot be shared with other members of your party.

Disabled Visitors

Parking places for disabled drivers are located in the centre of St Helier and St Peter Port and close to major tourist attractions, and you can use your Orange Badge on the islands. There are public toilets equipped for disabled users all over the islands, fitted with Radar locks – to use them you need your badge and key, or you can hire one from the Visitor Centres (*see* **Tourist Information**). Many visitors to the Channel Islands are elderly and so disabled facilities in shops and hotels, at tourist sights and on public transport tend to be good. The Visitor Centres also publish useful leaflets detailing special amenities on the islands.

Driving

To drive your own car in the Channel Islands, you must carry a Certificate of Insurance or International Green Card and a valid driving licence. A nationality plate must be displayed on the back of the vehicle. Cars are allowed only on Jersey, Guernsey and Alderney (Herm and Sark are traffic-free). Note that most petrol stations close on Sundays, especially in low season.

In general, many roads on the islands are narrow, with high banks or walls and few passing places. Visibility is poor at many junctions, and lanes are used by cyclists, horse-riders, tractors and pedestrians, as well as cars. Care is necessary at all times, and there are certain rules that are peculiar to the islands:

• Traffic drives on the left.
• The maximum speed is 64kph/40mph in Jersey, 56kph/35mph in Guernsey and Alderney. In towns it is 40kph/25mph, and in Green Lanes (which are clearly sign-posted) it is only 24kph/15mph.
• A yellow line across the junction of a minor road means you must stop and give way to traffic on the major road. A yellow arrow on the road warns of a junction ahead and indicates priority for traffic using these roads.
• Many junctions have a filter-in-turn system, marked by a cross-hatched yellow box painted in the road. At these junctions, all vehicles have equal priority and you take turns to enter the junction. You must not enter the box until your exit is clear.

• A single yellow line along the side of the road means no parking at any time.

Parking: On Jersey, parking is generally free, except in St Helier where you may park for the period of time indicated by the roadside sign (in central streets this may be for as little as 20 minutes, whereas further from the centre street parking is allowed for 1 or 2 hours). First you must buy paycards from shops and garages displaying the paycard symbol. When you park, scratch off the date and time to show when you arrived at the parking place, leaving the card visible in the car.

On Guernsey and Alderney all street parking is free, but you must use a parking disk to show the time you arrived, and you must not exceed the time limit shown on the street signs. Disks are supplied with hire cars or available free from the Visitor Centre in St Peter Port (*see* **Tourist Information**).

Electric Current

The voltage in the Channel Islands is 240volts AC and UK-style plugs, with three square-pins, are used.

Embassies *see* Consulates

Emergencies

The emergency telephone numbers are the same as those

Farmer and cows, Jersey.

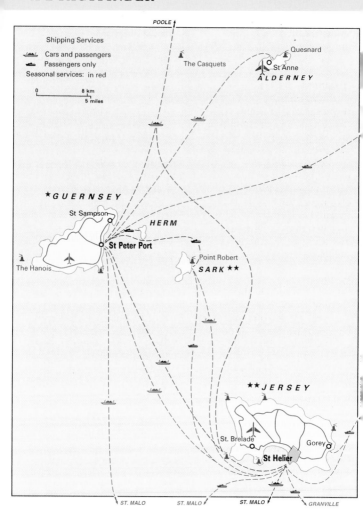

Ferry services within the Channel Islands

in the UK. ☎ **999** for police, ambulance, fire brigade or coastal rescue services.

Etiquette

Easy-going manners are the norm in the Channel Islands, though the islands of Herm and Sark have certain rules designed to preserve the peace on these tranquil islands. Pets must be kept under control, plants must not be picked, dropping litter is seriously frowned upon, and it is illegal to play transistor radios, ghetto-blasters or the like in public.

Excursions

Whichever island in the Channel Islands you decide to use as a base, it is always tempting to visit the others, if only for comparison's sake. If island-hopping appeals, then make Guernsey your base: from here it is a 20-minute ferry hop to Herm, and a 45-minute cruise to Sark. Jersey and Alderney are each a 15-minute flight away, or an hour by catamaran. Jersey and Guernsey both have frequent daily ferry departures for Channel ports in northern France and southern England. Ferries operate mainly in the high season (1 April to 30 September) with more limited services, very much dependent on the weather, at other times of year. For timetables, prices and advance bookings, contact the following:

Herm: Travel Trident operates 250-seater catamarans from St Peter Port to Herm, with departures at roughly 45-minute intervals throughout the day in high season ☎ **01481 721379**.

Sark: From Jersey, both Condor Ferries, ☎ **01534 872240**, and Emeraude Lines, ☎ **01534 66566**, operate a 45-minute catamaran service to Sark daily (except Sunday) from Elizabeth Harbour, St Helier. From Guernsey, the Isle of Sark Shipping Company, ☎ **01481 724059**, provides day-long excursions to Sark, with the options of including lunch, a 2-hour carriage ride, and entry to the Seigneurie Gardens in the ticket price.

Jersey/Guernsey: For day excursions from Jersey to Guernsey or vice versa, contact Emeraude Lines: Guernsey ☎ **01481 711414**; Jersey ☎ **01534 66566**; or Condor Ferries: Guernsey ☎ **01481 726121**; Jersey ☎ **01534 872240**.

France day trips: The following ferry companies all operate day trips to St-Malo from St Helier and St Peter Port, with guided onward transport by coach, if you wish, to Dinard, Mont St Michel, Dinan or St-Servan. Emeraud Lines also have day crossings to Carteret and Granville, on the Cotentin Peninsula, in Normandy. Contact Condor Ferries: Guernsey ☎ 01481 726121; Jersey ☎ 01534 872240; or Emeraude Lines: Guernsey ☎ 01481 711414; Jersey ☎ 01534 66566.

Air transport: Flights between Alderney, Guernsey and Jersey, Southampton, Caen and Dinard are provided by 16-seater Trislander planes ☎ 01481 822886 (Jersey) ☎ 01481 723474 (Guernsey).

Health

Reciprocal health agreements exist between the Channel Islands and a number of countries, including Australia, France, New Zealand and the UK, which means that hospital emergency and outpatient services are provided free to nationals of these countries. All doctors and dentists are in private practice and you will be charged the full cost of treatment and medicines if you use their services as a private patient, so holiday medical insurance is recommended. Remember to keep receipts to make your claim on your return home.

Outpatient emergency services are available at: **Jersey General Hospital**, Gloucester Street, St Helier ☎ 01534 725241. **Pier Steps Surgery** (in the basement of Boots the Chemist), High Street, St Peter Port, Guernsey ☎ 01481 711237. **The Island Medical Centre**, Ollivier Street, St Anne, Alderney ☎ 01481 822077.

Information see Tourist Information Offices

Language

English is spoken throughout the Channel islands and is the official language for government, law and education. A few islanders are bilingual, speaking the old Norman-French dialects of Jersey and Guernsey.

Laundry

Self-service coin-operated laundries are found in St Helier and St Peter Port, and most hotels offer a laundry service.

Lost Property

Inform your hotel or tour

operator, who will help you contact the police to report lost or stolen property. You will need an official report form from the police if you intend to make an insurance claim. The States of Guernsey Police Force has a well-run lost property department ☎ **01481 725111**.

Maps

Excellent free maps and guides (with up-to-date opening times) are given out by car hire firms and hotels. Alternatively, they can be obtained from the Visitor Centres (*see* **Tourist Information**). For walking and cycling, more detailed maps are available from the Visitor Centres and bookshops.

Medical Care *see* Health

Money *see* Banks

Newspapers

All the major UK and European newspapers and magazines are available from newsagents and bookshops in St Helier and St Peter Port, as well as many garage shops, usually on the day of publication (though as they are flown in from the UK they may be delayed by fog). Local newspapers are excellent for up-to-date nightlife and entertainment listings, and news of festivals and events.

Opening Hours

Shops: Most are open Mon-Fri, 9.30am-5.30pm, and Saturday 9.30am-4pm. Markets and some shops are closed on Thursday afternoons (Wednesday on Alderney), and bigger stores open later on Friday evenings. From mid-July to the end of August many more shops open late (until 7pm daily) and on Sunday, though Sunday opening is not yet widespread outside St Helier. Convenience stores attached to garages open much longer hours, and on Sunday.

Pharmacies: Chemists observe the same hours as shops. Notices posted on the doors will tell you where to find the nearest late-opening duty chemist.

Museums and monuments: These are generally open weekends in winter and daily from 1 April to 31 October. The usual core hours are 9.30am-5.30pm, with some variations. Note that many tourist attractions close from October to April.

Photography

Clear light and brilliant sunshine attract artists to the Channel Islands and account for its flourishing cut-flower trade. For the photographer, it means high-speed film and sunlight filters to make the best of the islands' scenery.

Police

Police maintain a low profile on the islands. They are courteous and helpful to visitors, though traffic wardens are very vigilant and will issue penalty notices to those who overstay their parking time, regardless of whether they are locals or visitors.

Post Offices

Jersey and Guernsey operate their own postal services and issue their own postage stamps, and each of the main post offices has a visitor centre geared to philatelists, with displays of commemorative issues. Jersey's main post office is in Broad Street, St Helier, and Guernsey's is in Smith Street, St Peter Port. You must use local stamps for mail posted on the islands; UK stamps are not valid, and neither are Guernsey stamps on Jersey, or vice versa.

Public Holidays

New Year's Day: 1 January
Good Friday and Easter
    Monday
May Day: first Monday in May

Liberation Day: 9 May
Spring Bank Holiday: last
    Monday in May
Late Summer Bank Holiday:
    last Monday in August
Christmas Day: 25 December
Boxing Day: 26 December

Religion

The Channel islands have a long history of dissent, and most Nonconformist Christian denominations have places of worship on the islands, as well as Roman Catholic and Anglican churches. Details of all church services are available from the Visitor Centres (*see* **Tourist Information**).

Smoking

Smoking is increasingly discouraged in public places, and many hotels and restaurants have no-smoking designated areas. A *Guide to Smoke-Free Eating and Drinking in the Channel Islands* is available from the Visitor Centres (*see* **Tourist Information**).

Telephones

Telephone kiosks are widely distributed and easy to use, either with cash or telephone cards. Telephone cards are sold by newsagents and in many general stores. Those issued by the Jersey Telephone Company cannot be used in

Guernsey Bailiwick, and vice versa.

To dial any location in the UK, you just dial the area code and number. To dial outside the UK, you need to dial the international access code (00) and the country code, followed by the area code, omitting the initial 0.

Time Difference
Like the UK, the Channel Islands observe Greenwich Mean Time from the last Sunday in October until the last Sunday in March, and Summer Time (GMT plus one hour) for the remainder of the year.

Tipping
A service charge of 10 to 15 per cent is added to the bill in more up-market restaurants. Otherwise, it is normal to give small change – about 10 per cent of the bill – to taxi drivers and waiters.

Toilets
On the whole, toilets in the Channel Islands are easy to find. There are public toilets close to most beaches and car parks, at all tourist attractions, cafés and restaurants, and in public buildings, as well as on the streets of St Helier and St Peter Port. The standard of cleanliness is usually high, though you may want to carry your own emergency supplies of toilet paper.

Tourist Information
The Visitor Centres on the Channel Islands are excellent and are well worth contacting in advance of your visit for free guides to accommodation, eating out, events and attractions. On arrival, head first for

Shrimping in Côbo Bay, Guernsey.

the Visitor Centres for leaflets on local attractions, walking and cycling guides, maps, and information on everything from brass band concerts in public parks, to craft demonstrations or participatory sports.

Jersey Tourism, Liberation Square, St Helier, Jersey JE1 1BB, ☎ 01534 500777, fax: 01534 500808, web site: http://www.jersey.gov.uk
States of Guernsey Tourist Board, PO Box 23, North Esplanade, St Peter Port, Guernsey GY1 3AN, ☎ 01481 723555 (accommodation), 01481 723552 (general enquiries), fax: 014811 714951, web site: http://tourism.guernsey.net

Although the Guernsey Visitor Centre handles enquiries about Herm, Sark and Alderney, each island has its own small Visitor Centre:

Sark Tourist Information Centre, Harbour Hill, Sark GY9 0S, ☎ 01481 832345, fax: 01481 832483.
Alderney Tourism Information Centre, Victoria Street, St Anne ☎ 01481 823737, fax: 01481 822436.
Herm Island Administration Office Herm GY1 3HR ☎ 01481 722377, fax: 01481 700334.

Transport

Jersey, Guernsey and Alderney all have good and frequent bus services reaching all parts of the islands and serving the leading visitor attractions, so that you could tour the islands entirely by public transport if you wished. Timetables can be obtained from the Visitor Centres. An Explorer ticket allows you unlimited travel for the duration of the ticket.

Taxis are also easy to find. They can be picked up at ranks in St Helier and St Peter Port, or you can order one by phone.

TV and Radio

Most of the islands' TV and radio sets are tuned in to UK channels, all of which are available. There are also local TV and radio stations broadcasting local news, traffic and weather reports. The better hotels also offer satellite TV channels.

Water

Tap water is drinkable and pleasant to taste. You will be served with mineral water (still or fizzy) if you order water in a pub, café or restaurant.

Youth Hostels

There are no youth hostels in the Channel Islands.

INDEX

Alderney 9, 91-95
  Braye Bay 94
  Braye Harbour 94
  Burhou Island 95
  Corblets Bay 92
  Fort Albert 93
  Fort Hommeaux Florains 93
  Fort Quesnard 93
  Hammond Memorial 94
  Quesnard lighthouse 92, 93
  railway 91-92, 93
  St Anne 94-95
    museum 95
  Telegraph Bay 95
  The Shed 94

Battle of Flowers 79, 96, 97, 98
Battle of Jersey 14, 15, 29, 31, 50
beaches 20, 22, 78

Durrell, Gerald 5, 60-61

ferry services 120, 121
food 5

Green Lanes 5, 19, 45
Guernsey 8-9, 62-81
  Bailiwick of 8-9
  beaches 78
  Bordeaux Harbour 81
  Brooklands Farm Implements Museum 78
  Côbo Bay 78
  Creux ès Faies dolmen 75
  Fermain Bay 70
  Fort Grey 74, 75
  German Occupation Museum 72, 73
  German Underground Military Hospital 78
  Guernsey Bird Gardens 78-79
  Guernsey Clockmakers 78
  Guernsey Folk Museum 22, 79
  Guernsey Freesia Centre 80, 108
  Guernsey Woodcarvers 76, 77
  Hanging Strawberry Farm 76
  Icart Point 73
  Jerbourg Point 70
  L'Ancresse Common 80

La Gran'mère du Chimquière 71-72
Ladies Bay 80
Le Déhus 81
Le Friquet: the Centre of Attractions 80
Le Trépied 76
Les Fouaillages 11, 80
Lihou Island 75
Little Chapel 77
Martello Towers 15
Moulin Huet Pottery 70, 72, 107
Moulin Huet Bay 22,72
Oatlands Craft Centre 79, 80, 107
Petit Bot Bay 23
Pleinmont Tower 74
Priory of St Mary 75
Rocquaine Bay 74-75
Saumarez Park 22, 79
Sausmarez Manor 71
Shipwreck Museum 75
St Apolline's Chapel 76
St Martin's Church 71
St Peter Port 22, 62-67
  Aquarium 64-65
  Candie Gardens 62, 67
  Castle Cornet 13, 22, 63, 65
  Guernsey Information Centre 62
  Guernsey Museum and Art Gallery 22, 67, 68
  harbour 62, 63, 65
  Hauteville House 22, 66, 68
  La Valette Underground Military Museum 64, 66
  markets 66
  Maritime Museum 11, 64
  Militia Museum 64
  Royal Court House 67
  Town Church 63
St Sampson 81
St Saviour's Tunnels 76
Telephone Museum 80
Vazon Bay 78

Herm 9, 82-84
  Belvoir Bay 83
  Jethou 83
  Le Grand Monceau 83
  Manoir Village 83
  Manor 83
  Oyster Rock 82
  Pierre aux Rats 82
  Rosière 82
  Sauzebourge Point 83
  Shell Beach 82, 83
  St Tugal's Chapel 83
Hugo, Victor 68-69

Jersey 6-8, 24-61
  Bailiwick of 6-8
  Battle of the Flowers Museum 59
  beaches 20
  Belle Hougue 7, 56
  Bonne Nuit Bay 56
  Bouley Bay 56
  Channel Islands Military Museum 59
  Corbière lighthouse 52, 53, 114
  Corbière Point 52
  Devil's Hole 20, 56
  Eric Young Orchid Foundation 45, 46
  Faldouet Dolmen 10, 40
  Fine Gems and Craft Centre 107
  Fort Regent Leisure Centre 108
  Frances Le Sueur Centre 59
  German Underground Hospital 20, 48
  Gorey 38-39, 40
  Grève de Lecq 57
  Grosnez Castle 58
  Grosnez Point 20, 58
  Hamptonne Country Life Museum 21, 46-47
  Island Centre Stone 46
  Jersey Butterfly Centre 57
  Jersey Flower Centre 57
  Jersey Motor Museum 50
  Jersey Pottery 39, 105, 107
  Jersey Zoo 21, 56, 60-61
  Jerusalem Chapel 41
  Kempt Tower 59
  La Cotte Cave 9, 58
  La Hougue Bie 11, 20, 41
    Archaeology Museum 41
    Geology Museum 41
    Neolithic hut 41
    communications bunker 41
  La Mare Vineyards 56
  La Roque 111
  Lavender Farm 54, 108
  Les Mielles 59
  Little Loft Gallery and Turnery 45
  Living Legend 50
  Mont Orgueil Castle 20, 21, 39, 40
  Moulin de Quetivel 49
  Noirmont Point 54
  North Coast Visitor Centre 57
  Our Lady of the Dawn Chapel 41

INDEX

Pallot Heritage Steam
  Museum 46, 47
Photographic Museum 44
Plémont Bay 58
Portelet Bay 53, 54
Queen's Valley Reservoir 40
Royal Bay of Grouville 21,
  39
Rozel 55, 57
Samarès Manor 38
Shell Garden 54-55
Sir Francis Cook Gallery 44
Sorel 56
St Aubin's Fort 54
St Brelade's Bay 52
  Fishermen's Chapel 12, 53
St Brelade's Church 53
St Clement's Bay 39
St Helier 24-37
  Albert Pier 25
  Beresford Market 33
  Central Market 32
  Elizabeth Castle 13, 20,
    35-37
  Fort Regent 25, 30
  harbour 24, 28
  Jardins de la Mer 35
  Jersey Occupation Tapestry

  Gallery 21, 26
Jersey Museum 9, 21, 28,
  29
Le Petit Train 30
Liberation Square 25
Maritime Museum 21, 26,
  27
  Occupation Museum 37
Opera House 35
Parish Church 29
Royal Square 31
Royal Court House 31
Salle paroissiale (Town
  Hall) 34
shopping 32
States Chambers 31-32
St Matthew's Church (Glass
  Church) 49
St Ouen's Bay 50, 51
St Peter's Valley 50
St Peter's Bunker Museum
  50
St Peter's Church 50
St Saviour's Church 44
Treasures of the Earth 59
Wolf's Cave 56

Lillie Langtry 28, 42-43, 44

Occupation 15-16, 26-27, 37,
  48, 49, 59, 64, 73, 78, 88

Peirson, Major Francis 14-15,
  29, 31
prehistoric remain 9-11, 20

Sark 9, 85-91
  Creux Harbour 85
  Derrible Bay 91
  Dixcart Bay 91
  Grande Grève 90, 91
  Great Sark 85
  La Collinette 86
  La Coupée 4, 23, 85, 89, 90
  La Seigneurie 23, 88
  Little Sark 85
  Maseline Harbour 85
  Port du Moulin 23, 90
  Prison 87
  Sark Occupation Museum
    88
  St Peter's Church 88
  Venus Pool 91
  Window in the Rock 90
Second World War 5, 13, 20,
  64